W9-CFB-603

Primary Source Accounts of the
War of 1812

HELEN KOUTRAS BOZONELIS

MyReportLinks.com Books

an imprint of

Enslow Publishers, Inc.
Box 398, 40 Industrial Road
Berkeley Heights, NJ 07922
USA

To my husband, Ted, and to our children, Justin and Lia; and to the memory of my parents, Andrew and Evangelia Koutras.

MyReportLinks.com Books, an imprint of Enslow Publishers, Inc. MyReportLinks® is a registered trademark of Enslow Publishers, Inc.

Copyright © 2006 by Enslow Publishers, Inc.

Library of Congress Cataloging-in-Publication Data

Bozonelis, Helen Koutras.
   Primary source accounts of the War of 1812 / Helen Koutras Bozonelis.
      p. cm. — (America's wars through primary sources)
   Includes bibliographical references and index.
   ISBN 1-59845-006-9
   1. United States—History—War of 1812—Sources—Juvenile literature.
   I. Title. II. Series.
   E354.B69 2006
   973.5'2—dc22

                                        2005035206

Printed in the United States of America

10 9 8 7 6 5 4 3 2 1

To Our Readers:
Through the purchase of this book, you and your library gain access to the Report Links that specifically back up this book.
The Publisher will provide access to the Report Links that back up this book and will keep these Report Links up to date on **www.myreportlinks.com** for five years from the book's first publication date.
We have done our best to make sure all Internet addresses in this book were active and appropriate when we went to press. However, the author and the Publisher have no control over, and assume no liability for, the material available on those Internet sites or on other Web sites they may link to.
The usage of the MyReportLinks.com Books Web site is subject to the terms and conditions stated on the Usage Policy Statement on **www.myreportlinks.com.**
A password may be required to access the Report Links that back up this book. The password is found on the bottom of page 4 of this book.
Any comments or suggestions can be sent by e-mail to comments@myreportlinks.com or to the address on the back cover.

Photo Credits: Archives of Ontario, Canada, pp. 52, 68, 101; *Battle of Lake Erie* by William Henry Powell (1823–1879) Oil on canvas, 1873; U.S. Senate Collection, p. 1; City of Hamilton, Ontario, p. 26; Courtesy of the State Archives of Michigan, p. 54; Department of the Navy, Naval Historical Center, pp. 36, 76, 88; Enslow Publishers, Inc., pp. 8, 44; Galafilm.com, p. 78; H. A. Ogden, *Uniforms of the United States Army, 1774–1889, in Full Color,* originally published in 1890 by the Quartermaster General of the Army of the United States, as *Uniform of the Army of the United States, Illustrated, From 1774 to 1889.* Republished 1998, © Dover Publications, p. 56; Hillsdale College, p. 34; James Madison University, p. 42; Lester S. Levy Collection of Sheet Music, p. 90; Library of Congress, pp. 3, 7, 13, 15, 19, 20, 24, 37, 59, 62, 84, 94, 96; MyReportLinks.com Books, p. 4; National Archives and Records Administration, pp. 22, 74, 109; Ohio History Central, p. 23; The AmericanPresident.org, p. 12; The Mariners' Museum, pp. 46, 86; The National Park Service, p. 111; The White House Historical Association, p. 103; U.S. Brig *Niagara*, p. 39; United States Army Center of Military History, pp. 35, 61, 64; Upper Canada History, p. 98; Virginia Center for Digital History, p. 10.

Cover Photo: *Battle of Lake Erie* by William Henry Powell (1823–1879) Oil on canvas, 1873; U.S. Senate Collection.

Every effort has been made to locate all copyright holders of material used in this book. If any errors or omissions have occurred, please contact us at www.myreportlinks.com. We will try to make corrections in future editions.

CONTENTS

MyReportLinks.com Books
Great Books, Great Links, Great for Research!

The Internet sites featured in this book can save you hours of research time. These Internet sites—we call them **"Report Links"**—are constantly changing, but we keep them up to date on our Web site.

When you see this "Approved Web Site" logo, you will know that we are directing you to a great Internet site that will help you with your research.

Give it a try! Type http://www.myreportlinks.com into your browser, click on the series title and enter the password, then click on the book title, and scroll down to the Report Links listed for this book.

The Report Links will bring you to great source documents, photographs, and illustrations. MyReportLinks.com Books save you time, feature Report Links that are kept up to date, and make report writing easier than ever! A complete listing of the Report Links can be found on pages 112–113 at the back of the book.

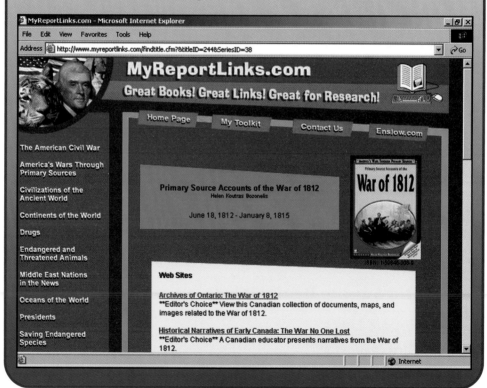

Please see "To Our Readers" on the copyright page for important information about this book, the MyReportLinks.com Web site, and the Report Links that back up this book.

Please enter PWE1888 if asked for a password.

WHAT ARE PRIMARY SOURCES?

In Camp, near raisin River, Jan. 16, 1813.

Dear Susan:

I have only time to inform you that we expect to have a battle tomorrow with the British and Indians. . . . It may be possible I may fall in battle and my only boy must know that his father, next to God, loves his country, and is now risking his life in defending that country against a barbarous and cruel enemy.

—Captain James C. Price, a Kentucky militiaman.

The young soldier who wrote these words never dreamed that they would be read by anyone but his wife. They were not intended to be read as a history of the War of 1812. But his words—and the words of others that have come down to us through scholars or were saved over generations by family members—are unique resources. Historians call such writings primary source documents. As you read this book, you will find other primary source accounts of the war written by the men who fought it. Their letters home reflect their thoughts, their dreams, their fears, and their longing for loved ones. Some of them speak of the excitement of battle, while others mention the everyday boredom of day-to-day life in camp.

But the story of a war is not only the story of the men and women in service. This book also contains diary entries, newspaper accounts, official documents, speeches, and songs of the war years. They reflect the opinions of those who were not in battle but who were still affected by the war. All of these things as well as photographs and art are primary sources—they were created by people who participated in, witnessed, or were affected by the events of the time.

Many of these sources, such as letters and diaries, are a reflection of personal experience. Others, such as newspaper accounts, reflect the mood of the time as well as the opinions of the papers' editors. All of them give us a unique insight into history as it happened. But it is also important to keep in mind that each source reflects its author's biases, beliefs, and background. Each is still someone's interpretation of an event.

Some of the primary sources in this book will be easy to understand; others may not. Their authors came from a different time and were products of different backgrounds and levels of education. So as you read their words, you will see that some of those words may be spelled differently than we would spell them. And some of their stories may be written without the kinds of punctuation we are used to seeing. Each source has been presented as it was originally written, but wherever a word or phrase is unclear or might be misunderstood, an explanation has been added.

TIME LINE OF THE WAR OF 1812

1807—JUNE 22: British vessel the HMS *Leopard* attacks the USS *Chesapeake* and impresses, or seizes, American sailors.

—NOVEMBER 11: Great Britain enforces the Orders in Council to restrict American shipping.

—DECEMBER 22: United States Congress passes the Embargo Act to end trade with Great Britain.

1811—NOVEMBER 7: General William Henry Harrison defeats Shawnee chief Tecumseh and his brother, known as the Prophet, at the Battle of Tippecanoe.

1812—JUNE 18: The United States declares war on Great Britain.

—AUGUST 16: General William Hull surrenders Fort Detroit without a fight.

—AUGUST 19: USS *Constitution* captures HMS *Guerrière.*

—OCTOBER 13: Britain wins Battle of Queenston Heights in Canada; British major general Isaac Brock is killed.

1813—JANUARY 22: Kentucky militia are massacred at River Raisin (Frenchtown).

—APRIL 27: Americans capture and torch York, the capital of Upper Canada.

—JUNE 1: HMS *Shannon* captures USS *Chesapeake.*

—SEPTEMBER 10: Commodore Oliver Perry wins the Battle of Lake Erie.

—OCTOBER 5: General William Henry Harrison defeats British and American Indians on the Thames River, in Canada; Tecumseh is killed.

1814—SPRING: British Royal Navy sets up a blockade of American ports.

—MARCH 27: Andrew Jackson defeats Creek Indians at Horseshoe Bend in Alabama.

—JULY 5: Americans win Battle of Chippewa.

—JULY 25: Battle of Lundy's Lane, near Niagara in Canada, ends in a draw.

—AUGUST 24: British capture Washington, D.C., and burn the Capitol and President's House (the White House).

—SEPTEMBER 11: Commodore Thomas MacDonough defeats the British fleet at the Battle of Lake Champlain (Plattsburgh, New York).

—SEPTEMBER 13–14: British bombard Fort McHenry, in Baltimore.

—DECEMBER 24: United States and Britain sign the Treaty of Ghent in Belgium.

1815—JANUARY 8: Andrew Jackson defeats British at Battle of New Orleans.

—FEBRUARY 17: President James Madison declares the end of the War of 1812.

Andrew Jackson at the Battle of New Orleans.

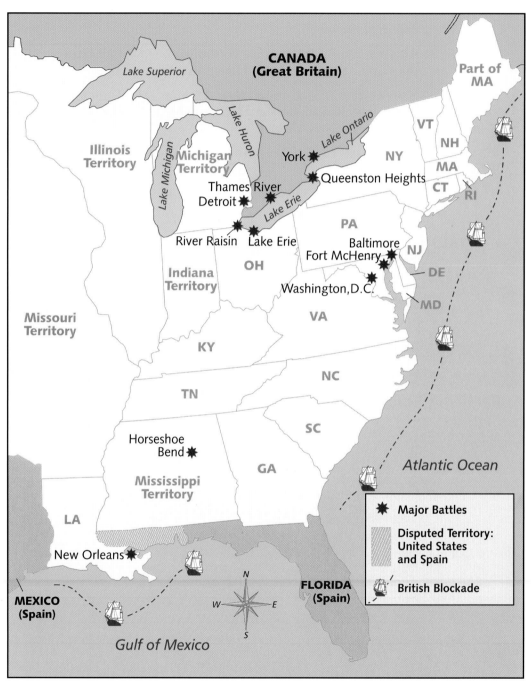

CANADA
(Great Britain)

Lake Superior

Part of
MA

Lake Huron

Lake Ontario

VT

NH

Illinois
Territory

Michigan
Territory

York

NY

MA

Queenston Heights

CT

Lake Michigan

Thames River
Detroit

Lake Erie

RI

River Raisin   Lake Erie

PA

Baltimore
Fort McHenry

NJ

Indiana
Territory

OH

Washington, D.C.

DE

Missouri
Territory

VA

MD

KY

Atlantic Ocean

NC

TN

SC

Horseshoe
Bend

GA

Mississippi
Territory

LA

New Orleans

N

MEXICO
(Spain)

W   E

FLORIDA
(Spain)

S

Gulf of Mexico

★ Major Battles

Disputed Territory:
United States
and Spain

British Blockade

▲ This map shows where some of the major battles of the War of 1812 were fought.

WASHINGTON BURNING

When the blazing sun rose on the morning of August 24, 1814, few residents of Washington City (as Washington, D.C., the nation's capital, was known) suspected the drama that was about to unfold. Perhaps Dolley Payne Madison, the wife of President James Madison, had a hunch. She pushed aside the drapes that hung in the President's House and gazed along Pennsylvania Avenue. Just the day before, Mrs. Madison had written to her sister Lucy:

> My husband left me yesterday morning . . . beseeching me to take care of myself, and of the cabinet papers, public and private. . . . he desires I should be ready at a moment's warning to enter my carriage and leave the city; that the enemy seemed stronger than had been reported and that it might happen that they would reach the city, with intention to destroy it.[1]

To be safe, Dolley Madison packed official papers into several small trunks. Her beloved husband, whom she affectionately called Jemmy, would return home soon and she would feel secure. Little did any of them realize that this day, August 24, 1814, would be one of the darkest days in the early history of the United States.

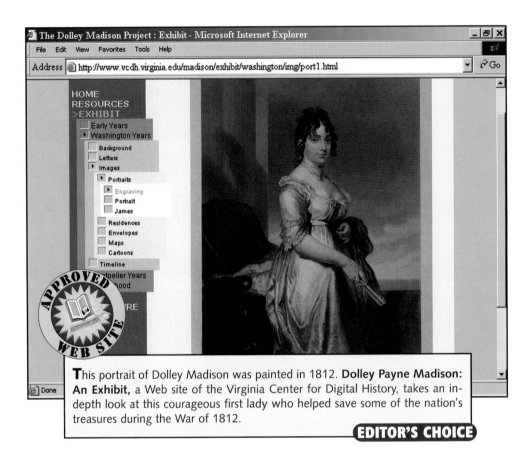

The Dolley Madison Project : Exhibit - Microsoft Internet Explorer

File   Edit   View   Favorites   Tools   Help

Address http://www.vcdh.virginia.edu/madison/exhibit/washington/img/port1.html   Go

HOME
RESOURCES
>EXHIBIT
  Early Years
  ▸ Washington Years
    Background
    Letters
    ▸ Images
      ▸ Portraits
        ▸ Engraving
        Portrait
        James
    Residences
    Envelopes
    Maps
    Cartoons
  Timeline
  ...ontpelier Years
  ...hood
  ...RE

This portrait of Dolley Madison was painted in 1812. **Dolley Payne Madison: An Exhibit,** a Web site of the Virginia Center for Digital History, takes an in-depth look at this courageous first lady who helped save some of the nation's treasures during the War of 1812.

EDITOR'S CHOICE

▶ Out for Revenge

No one really believed the capital of the United States would be the target of an attack. It was not important from a military point of view. Washington City was a muddy village built on the banks of the Potomac River. About eight thousand people lived there. A former first lady, Abigail Adams, once wrote: "It is a beautiful spot, capable of every improvement."[2]

But the nation was at war again with Great Britain, and the British commander, Admiral

Alexander Cochrane, issued orders to his men to ravage American cities, directing them to "destroy and lay waste such towns and districts upon the coasts as [you may] find assailable [defenseless]."[3]

Such orders were gleefully carried out by Vice Admiral George Cockburn, a British commander who terrorized towns along Chesapeake Bay. Cockburn despised the United States. He had not forgotten how American forces had just sixteen months earlier destroyed York, the capital of Upper Canada. Cockburn craved revenge. Early in August, British warships sailed into Chesapeake Bay.

Warning Signs Ignored

President Madison and his government did not pay attention to warnings of an invasion. He had penned a letter to Dolley about the British that showed his lack of concern:

> The last & probably truest information is that they are not very strong, and are without cavilry [mounted troops] and artillery, and of course that they are not in a condition to strike at Washington. . . . I hope I shall be with you . . . perhaps later in the evening.
> Your devoted husband, J.M.[4]

The letter was dated Tuesday, August 23, 1814.

John Armstrong, the secretary of war, also did not believe the British would attack Washington City. He refused to strengthen the capital's defenses,

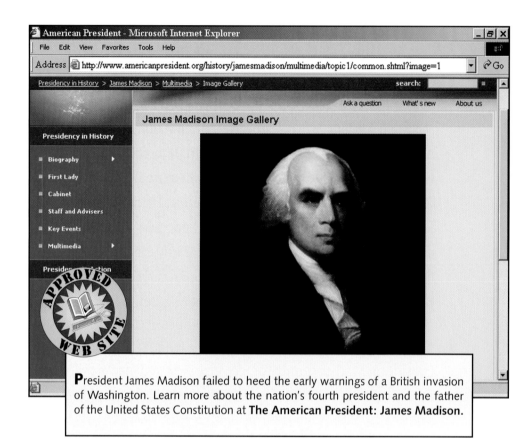

American President - Microsoft Internet Explorer

File   Edit   View   Favorites   Tools   Help

Address http://www.americanpresident.org/history/jamesmadison/multimedia/topic1/common.shtml?image=1   Go

Presidency in History > James Madison > Multimedia > Image Gallery   search:

Ask a question   What's new   About us

James Madison Image Gallery

Presidency in History

- Biography
- First Lady
- Cabinet
- Staff and Advisers
- Key Events
- Multimedia

President James Madison failed to heed the early warnings of a British invasion of Washington. Learn more about the nation's fourth president and the father of the United States Constitution at **The American President: James Madison.**

telling an officer, "They [British] would not come with such a fleet without meaning to strike somewhere. But they certainly will not come here! What the devil will they do here? No! No! Baltimore is the place, Sir. That is of so much more consequence [importance]."[5]

Even the *Daily National Intelligencer,* a Washington newspaper, downplayed the threat. On the morning of the invasion, the paper commented, "We feel assured that the number and bravery of our men, will afford complete protection to the city . . . These, and reinforcements every moment expected, added to our other forces, will secure the safety of the metropolis."[6]

The Bladensburg Races

Around midnight on August 23, President Madison received a note from James Monroe, his secretary of state, which carried this warning: "The enemy are in full march for Washington. . . . You had better remove the records."[7]

On the morning of August 24, President Madison received word that the British were on the march to Bladensburg, six miles north of Washington.

▲ The British invasion and burning of Washington was a huge embarrassment for the United States—and in particular for its chief executive. In this British cartoon from 1814, President Madison and John Armstrong, his secretary of war, are the objects of ridicule as they flee the capital.

American troops gathered to defend Bladensburg. Madison left his wife at the President's House, promising to return at three o'clock to enjoy a dinner party that included his cabinet, his administration's advisors. He and a few cabinet members rode off to the front lines to join the troops. The battle began around noon.

At about the same time and a few miles away, Dolley wrote to her sister Lucy: "Wednesday morng., twelve o'clock. Since sunrise I have been turning my spy glass in every direction and watching with unwearied anxiety, hoping to discern the approach of my dear husband and his friends. . . ."[8]

Back on the battlefield, the American troops tried to stop the British, but they were untrained and were no match for the skilled British troops led by General Robert Ross. The battle lasted almost three hours when the American troops panicked and fled for safety. The president and government officials galloped away to the mountains of Virginia. They fled so quickly that the retreat was nicknamed the Bladensburg Races.

A National Heroine

General Ross marched his five thousand worn-out British solders and marines to their target, Washington City, in stifling heat. News of the British advance caused panic in Washington. Homes were boarded up and emptied. The streets were crowded with men, women, and children throwing their

This daguerreotype of Mrs. Madison, an early photograph made on a silver or copper plate, was taken by Mathew Brady in 1848, a year before her death. Brady would go on to become famous for his Civil War photographs.

household furniture and possessions into carts and wagons and then fleeing the capital. Washington City became a ghost town—and it was left defenseless.

Back at the President's House, Dolley Madison brought her sister up to date in her running account:

Three O'clock. Will you believe it, my Sister? We have had a battle or skirmish near Bladensburg, and I am still here within sound of the cannon! Mr. Madison comes not; may God protect him! Two messengers covered with dust, come to bid me fly; but I wait for him.[9]

Dolley Madison had not finished packing, though. She was determined to leave nothing of value for the enemy. It was an extraordinary act of bravery. Among the treasures were a copy of the Declaration of Independence and boxes with presidential papers. She instructed her servants,

"If you can't save them, destroy them."[10] She refused to leave without the priceless portrait of George Washington that had been painted by Gilbert Stuart. "Save that picture, if possible," she ordered. "If not possible, destroy it: under no circumstances allow it to fall into the hands of the British."[11] Mrs. Madison had it pulled down from the dining-room wall, removed it from its frame, and rolled it up like a giant scroll.

She ended her letter to Lucy:

It is done . . . the precious portrait placed in the hands of two gentlemen of New York, for safe keeping. And now, dear sister, I must leave this house, or the retreating army will make me a prisoner in it, by filling up the road I am directed to take. When I shall again write you, or where I shall be tomorrow, I cannot tell!![12]

Paul Jennings, a fifteen-year-old African-American slave who was devoted to the Madisons, was with her. He described the scene:

All then was confusion. Mrs. Madison ordered her carriage, and passing through the dining-room, caught up what silver she could crowd into her old-fashioned reticule [purse], and then jumped into the chariot . . . The British were expected in a few minutes. . . . People were running in every direction.[13]

The Capitol in Flames

At eight o'clock that evening, Admiral Cockburn and General Ross led their forces into Washington. They marched down Maryland Avenue, at whose end stood the imposing United States Capitol. Cockburn wanted to teach the Americans a lesson. He decided to humiliate American citizens by flying the British flag over the Capitol.

British soldiers broke in and searched all the rooms. Inside one of the chambers, Cockburn came across Madison's personal leather-bound copy of the government's budget for the year 1810. He stole it as souvenir of his victory. Cockburn later inscribed on the inside cover "Taken in President's room in the Capitol, at the destruction of that building by the British, on the Capture of Washington 24th. August 1814," later adding "by Admiral Cockburn."[14]

Ross ordered his troops to set fire to the building. They piled up furniture and ripped out window frames, shutters, and doors and tossed them on the piles. They stacked this "firewood" in the rooms and torched it. The Supreme Court and the Library of Congress were also housed in the Capitol. The Capitol was burning—and with it, three thousand books.

The President's Palace Ablaze

Around 10:30 that evening, Ross marched his troops to the President's House, which they nicknamed the President's Palace. They entered the deserted mansion.

George Robert Gleig, an officer in the British Army, wrote an account of what happened next:

When the detachment, sent out to destroy Mr. Madison's house, entered his dining parlor, they found a dinner-table spread, and covers laid for forty guests. . . . everything was ready for the entertainment of a ceremonious party. . . . They sat down to it . . . and having satisfied their appetites . . . and partaken pretty freely of the wines, they finished by setting fire to the house which so liberally entertained them. [15]

The British looted the President's House before they torched it, snatching souvenirs for themselves. Cockburn made a toast "To little Jemmy" and stole an old hat that belonged to the president. General Ross poked through a desk drawer and uncovered a packet of letters that President Madison had written to his wife. He stuffed them into his pocket and later boasted, "My pocket is full of old Madison's love letters."[16]

Ross directed the arson. He went to the Oval Room and ordered his men to put the elegant furniture in a pile, to be used as firewood. Troops stacked sofas, chairs, drapes—even the pianoforte (an early form of piano), a favorite piece of the first lady. They lit the heap, and within fifteen minutes the President's House was engulfed in flames.

The British troops moved on and continued their spree of looting and burning. They torched public buildings and destroyed public property. Under strict

 *The President's House, as the White House was then known, is pictured after being burned by the British.*

orders, they were careful not to damage private homes. They set fires that turned the capital city into an inferno.

Across the way, American soldiers destroyed their own warships and blew up the Washington Navy Yard to prevent the British from capturing it. One Washington resident, Mrs. Mary Stockton Hunter, wrote a letter to her sister describing the horrors of the night:

> No pen can describe the apalling sound that our ears heard, and the sight that our eyes saw. We could see everything from the upper part of our house. . . . All the vessels of war on fire . . . the houses and stores in flames. . . . You never saw a drawing room so brilliantly lighted as the whole city was that night. Few thought

of going to bed—they spent the night in gazing on the fires, and lamenting the disgrace of the city.[17]

That evening, giant black clouds rolled in. A storm with violent winds ripped through the city, toppling trees and tearing roofs from homes. The driving rain lasted for two hours and drenched the fires. Captain Gleig, the British officer, later wrote: "A hurricane fell on the city. . . . It fairly lifted me out of the saddle, and the horse which I had been riding I never saw again."[18]

After the storm, the British withdrew from Washington and marched on to capture their next prize: Alexandria, Virginia.

▶ Return to the Capital

What had happened to President Madison? He and Mrs. Madison had been waiting for each other in

▲ The United States Capitol building after "the Conflagration of the 24th August" is depicted in this painting.

different places. They finally reunited in Virginia at Wiley's Tavern, a hotel located about twenty-seven miles west of Washington. The Madisons returned to the capital along with the residents who had fled for their lives. Upon their arrival, they discovered a charred wasteland.

A visitor to the White House, William Wirt, wrote to his wife on October 14:

> I went to look at the ruins of the President's house. The rooms which you saw, so richly furnished, exhibited nothing but unroofed naked walls, cracked, defaced and blackened with fire. . . . I called on the President. He looks miserably shattered and woebegone. In short, he looked heart broken.[19]

The first details of the invasion spread from town to town and throughout the country. The national mood became one of alarm and despair and then anger and indignation. The British had occupied the capital for about twenty-five hours, inflicting millions of dollars in damage. It was a day of national humiliation for the American people.

Why War?

What caused this large-scale British invasion of America's shores? Why were these two nations at war again? The story of the War of 1812 is one of a bloody confrontation in which Americans took up arms against the British and their Canadian and

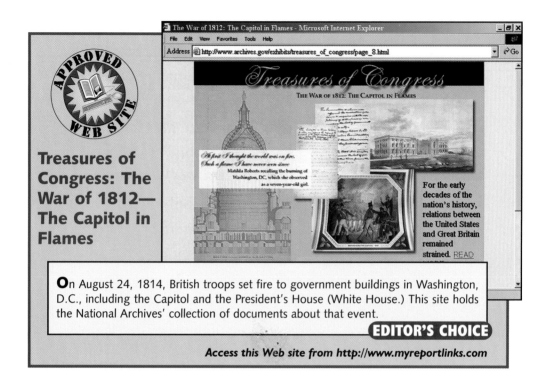

Treasures of Congress: The War of 1812— The Capitol in Flames

On August 24, 1814, British troops set fire to government buildings in Washington, D.C., including the Capitol and the President's House (White House.) This site holds the National Archives' collection of documents about that event.

EDITOR'S CHOICE

Access this Web site from http://www.myreportlinks.com

American Indian allies. It is also a story that can be told through the personal accounts of the men and women, soldiers and civilians, who faced danger and hardship during the war. Their reflections capture the drama of life that arose because of unresolved disagreements between the United States and Great Britain. Although it lasted only thirty months, the War of 1812 shaped the course of American history.

> **Chapter 2 ▶**

A BRIEF HISTORY OF THE WAR OF 1812

The War of 1812 has been called the forgotten war because it took place between two major conflicts in the history of the United States: the Revolutionary War and the Civil War. Historians have called it an unnecessary war, a mistake, and a

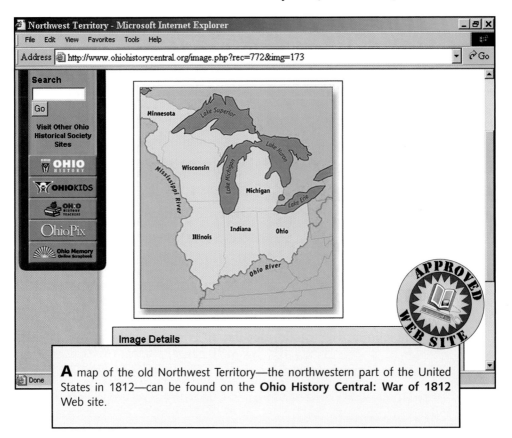

Image Details

A map of the old Northwest Territory—the northwestern part of the United States in 1812—can be found on the **Ohio History Central: War of 1812** Web site.

war that no one wanted. It also has been referred to as the Second War of Independence.

The story begins in the early 1800s. The United States was a young nation, enjoying a time of peace and growth. In 1812, there were about 7.5 million people living on land that stretched from New Hampshire south to the Gulf of Mexico and from the Atlantic Ocean west to the Rocky Mountains.[1] There were eighteen loosely joined states that made up the United States. Although the Treaty of Paris had ended the long, hard-fought Revolutionary War two decades earlier, there was still tension between the two nations over some unsettled business.

Control of the Northwest

The fight to control land in the Northwest Territory was a major issue. The territory consisted of what are the present-day states of Ohio, Michigan, Indiana, Wisconsin, and Illinois. Western settlers began streaming there, hungry

◁ William Henry Harrison's defeat of Tecumseh at Tippecanoe, in 1811, earned Harrison lasting fame. It also prompted Tecumseh to forge an alliance with the British during the War of 1812.

for more land and opportunity. Britain encouraged and armed American Indians to attack these settlers and keep them out.

By 1800, Tecumseh, a Shawnee from the Ohio Territory, had become a powerful leader of the northern Indian tribes. A tall, gallant figure, he wanted to preserve native lands and the traditional way of life. He and his brother, Tenskwatawa, who was known as the Prophet, led a confederation, or union, of tribes to stop settlers from moving west. Tecumseh founded a settlement called Prophetstown, on the banks of the Tippecanoe River in what is today Indiana. Tecumseh was also a fiery speaker who delivered impassioned speeches about the wrongs done to American Indians by white settlers.

> We are made miserable by the white people who are never satisfied and are always encroaching on our land. They have driven us from the great salt water, forced us over the mountains and would shortly push us into the lakes. We are determined to go no further. The only way to stop this is for all red men to unite in claiming a common right in the soil. No one tribe has a right to sell even to one another much less to strangers who demand all and will take no less. . . . Sell a country! Why not sell the air, the clouds, the great sea as well as the earth? Did not the Great Spirit make them all for the use of his children?[2]

Tecumseh's great enemy was William Henry Harrison, governor of the Indiana Territory. Harrison was alarmed about Tecumseh's increasing power, describing him as ". . . one of those uncommon geniuses, which spring up occasionally to produce revolutions. . . ."[3] In November 1811, Harrison led an army to Prophetstown and burned down the entire village at the Battle of Tippecanoe. As a result, Tecumseh and his followers decided to fight alongside the British in Canada during the war.

Border Disputes

Both the United States and Great Britain knew that whoever controlled the Great Lakes region controlled the West. After the Revolutionary War, Britain refused to give up forts scattered along the

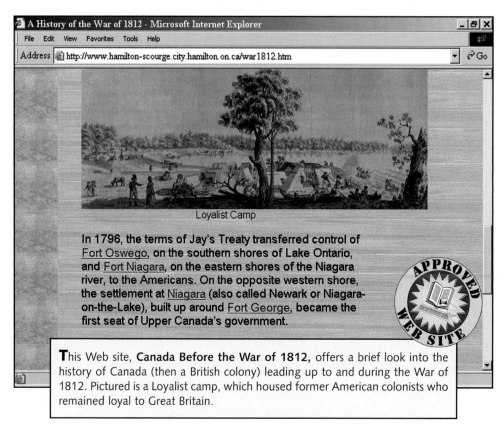

A History of the War of 1812 - Microsoft Internet Explorer

File   Edit   View   Favorites   Tools   Help

Address http://www.hamilton-scourge.city.hamilton.on.ca/war1812.htm

Loyalist Camp

In 1796, the terms of Jay's Treaty transferred control of Fort Oswego, on the southern shores of Lake Ontario, and Fort Niagara, on the eastern shores of the Niagara river, to the Americans. On the opposite western shore, the settlement at Niagara (also called Newark or Niagara-on-the-Lake), built up around Fort George, became the first seat of Upper Canada's government.

This Web site, **Canada Before the War of 1812,** offers a brief look into the history of Canada (then a British colony) leading up to and during the War of 1812. Pictured is a Loyalist camp, which housed former American colonists who remained loyal to Great Britain.

Great Lakes even though these were in American territory. This land was valuable for its fur trade routes, and Britain did not want to give up the money it made selling beaver and muskrat pelts in Europe. Border disputes erupted between the United States and Great Britain over Canada. In 1791, Britain had divided its colony in Canada into Lower Canada (now the province of Quebec) and Upper Canada (today, Ontario). Upper Canada was home to the United Empire Loyalists, who remained loyal subjects of the British crown when they fled the thirteen colonies during the American Revolution. Western settlers wanted to annex, or add, Canada to the United States. Canada's population at that time was about five hundred thousand.[4]

Impressment

There was another problem. On the seas, the British captured American ships and forced the sailors to serve in the Royal Navy. They considered people born in England or America during the Colonial period to be British subjects and required them to participate in military service, if needed. From 1796 until 1812, Britain had impressed, or taken by force, more than ten thousand American seamen. Americans became outraged when, in 1807, the *Leopard,* a British frigate, fired on the *Chesapeake,* an American frigate, and forced it to surrender. The British killed three sailors, wounded fourteen more, and seized four alleged deserters. Americans were furious and called for an embargo on British ships entering American ports.

There were other troubles on the seas. Great Britain and France were engaged in a long and costly war against each other. At first, the United States made huge profits by trading freely with both countries. By 1806, Britain and France were trying to destroy each other's trade. France declared a blockade to keep American ships from reaching Britain and ruin its economy. Likewise, the British passed a law that prevented the United States from trading with foreign countries unless it first bought a license from Britain. It was called the Orders in Council. Both Britain and France declared they would seize the cargo of any ships bound for the blockaded ports. In December 1807, the United States Congress passed the Embargo Act, which prohibited trade with other nations. This proved to be disastrous for America because shipping was the foundation of the American

APPROVED WEB SITE

The James Madison Center: War of 1812

Access this Web site from http://www.myreportlinks.com

This university site holds the archives of President James Madison, including letters and documents written by Madison during the years of the War of 1812.

EDITOR'S CHOICE

economy. Merchants, shippers, dockworkers, and sailors were hard hit as were the farmers who produced goods for foreign trade. Unemployment rose in seaport cities in New England and New York.

The Parties Involved

In 1812, Americans had a hard time figuring out what to do. As war loomed, some were against going to war with Great Britain, while others favored the coming combat. The United States was a nation divided.

President James Madison was considered a quiet intellectual. He was a well-read, thoughtful, and studious man who wanted to stay out of a war with Britain—or anyone. According to Madison, "Of all the enemies to public liberty war, is, perhaps, the most to be dreaded."[5]

The issue of war was hotly debated in Congress. On one hand, a group in Congress known as the War Hawks demanded war. The War Hawks were from the Republican party (a shortened name for the Democratic-Republican party, the forerunner to today's Democratic party) and came from the western and southern states. (Madison, a Virginian, also belonged to this party.) Henry Clay, from Kentucky, was one of the party's leaders. In a speech to the United States Senate on February 22, 1810, Clay declared, "The conquest of Canada is in our power. . . . I verily believe that the militia of Kentucky are alone competent to place Montreal and Upper Canada at your feet."[6]

On the other hand, members of the Federalist party, which was strongest in New York and the New England states, bitterly opposed what they had come to call "Mr. Madison's War." They hoped to continue sea trade with Britain because commerce was necessary for their survival. During the war, the people of New England even threatened to secede, or break away, from the United States. A few months after war began, the *Columbian Centinel,* a news-paper in Boston, ran an article titled "The New England Threat of Secession" that declared

> We have no more interest in waging this sort of war, at this period and under these circumstances. . . . The consequence of this state of things must then be, either that the Southern States must drag the Northern States farther into the war, or we must drag them out of it; or the chain will break. . . . It is an event we do not desire.[7]

What was Britain's attitude about war? On one hand, Britain's ruling monarch, King George III, did not have the resources to wage another war across the ocean. On the other hand, there were strong anti-American feelings in Britain left over from the Revolutionary War.

The British subjects in Upper Canada were also divided in their support. The United Empire Loyalists were keen on war. But the new emigrants from the

United States were sympathetic to their families in the United States and wanted to be left alone.

American Indians were unevenly divided on the war. A few native nations supported the United States, but most sided with Britain after the Battle of Tippecanoe.

Following months of heated debate, Congress declared war on Great Britain on June 18, 1812. It is ironic that at the same time, Britain agreed to stop attacking American vessels. Communication traveled slowly, and the news reached Washington City too late. The two nations drifted into war against each other, neither side wanting it.

▶ Unprepared for War

The United States Army and Navy were unprepared for war. They were no match for Britain, which was at the height of its military power. There were fewer than ten thousand regular soldiers enlisted in the United States Army. They were untrained; poorly clothed; poorly paid, receiving only eight dollars per month; and had to serve five years or the duration of the war. Daily rations were one and a quarter pounds of beef or salted pork, eight ounces of bread or flour, and four ounces of whiskey or rum.[8] The officers were either too old for combat or lacked the skills to win a war.

The United States was forced to depend on individual state militias made up of American citizens who would act as soldiers when needed. These

The Avalon Project at Yale Law School: The War of 1812

Access this Web site from http://www.myreportlinks.com

The text of the declaration that led to war between the United States and Great Britain in 1812 can be found on this Web site of the Avalon Project at Yale Law School.

militiamen were even more untrained and undisciplined than the regular soldiers. Moreover, they lacked sufficient weapons and served for only three months per year. Sometimes they were reluctant to fight or refused to cross a border and invade a foreign country. Unsanitary conditions led soldiers to become ill with dysentery, pneumonia, and typhus. Morale was understandably low.

The United States Navy had been almost entirely ignored since the Revolutionary War. It could barely handle its peacetime duties. It had about fifty ships and four thousand sailors. It was no match for the Royal Navy, which boasted more than 640 warships.[9] The *Times* of London ridiculed the American Navy, calling it a ". . . handful of fir-built frigates . . . manned by bastards and outlaws."[10]

Lacking ships and manpower, the United States was forced to encourage privateers, privately owned warships whose crews, also called privateers, seized merchant ships for prize money. Congress passed the Torpedo Act on March 3, 1813, making it lawful for anyone ". . . to burn, sink, or destroy, any British armed vessel of war . . . and . . . to use torpedoes, submarine instruments, or any other destructive machine. . . ." The prize: ". . . one-half the value of the armed vessel . . . and . . . one-half the value of her guns, cargo, tackle, and apparel."[11] Every sailor hoped to capture a rich enemy ship.

The Invasion of Canada

In 1812, the United States decided to invade Canada. American forces attacked on three fronts along the Great Lakes: Detroit, Niagara, and Lake Champlain. It was a daring plan—and all three attacks were failures.

In one of the most disgraceful blunders of the war, General William Hull, commander of the United States Army in the Northwest, called upon Canadians to surrender, warning them, "The army under my Command has invaded your Country. . . . I come to *find* enemies not to *make* them . . . this war, will be a war of extermination."[12] Just one month later, on August 16, 1812, it was Hull who surrendered to

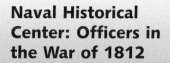

Naval Historical Center: Officers in the War of 1812

Access this Web site from http://www.myreportlinks.com

On this Web site from the Naval Historical Center, you can view a listing of all servicemen in the Navy and Marine Corps at the end of the War of 1812.

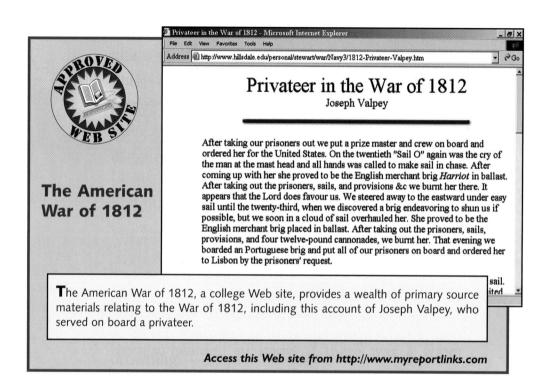

Privateer in the War of 1812 - Microsoft Internet Explorer

File   Edit   View   Favorites   Tools   Help

Address http://www.hillsdale.edu/personal/stewart/war/Navy3/1812-Privateer-Valpey.htm

Privateer in the War of 1812
Joseph Valpey

After taking our prisoners out we put a prize master and crew on board and ordered her for the United States. On the twentieth "Sail O" again was the cry of the man at the mast head and all hands was called to make sail in chase. After coming up with her she proved to be the English merchant brig *Harriot* in ballast. After taking out the prisoners, sails, and provisions &c we burnt her there. It appears that the Lord does favour us. We steered away to the eastward under easy sail until the twenty-third, when we discovered a brig endeavoring to shun us if possible, but we soon in a cloud of sail overhauled her. She proved to be the English merchant brig placed in ballast. After taking out the prisoners, sails, provisions, and four twelve-pound cannonades, we burnt her. That evening we boarded an Portuguese brig and put all of our prisoners on board and ordered her to Lisbon by the prisoners' request.

The American War of 1812

The American War of 1812, a college Web site, provides a wealth of primary source materials relating to the War of 1812, including this account of Joseph Valpey, who served on board a privateer.

Access this Web site from http://www.myreportlinks.com

Major General Isaac Brock, commander of the forces in Upper Canada. Hull gave up Fort Detroit and his two thousand troops to the British and their Indian allies without ever firing a shot. An article in the August 31, 1812, edition of the *New York Evening Post* blasted Hull: ". . . The army which has thus surrendered must be a gang of more cowardly poltroons than ever disgraced a country. A parallel to this melancholy defeat is not to be found in all history."[13] Hull was sentenced to death for cowardice but was later pardoned.

On the second front, American troops led by Major General Stephen Van Rensselaer crossed the Niagara River to attack Queenston Heights, in

Canada. On October 13, he surrendered to the British because the militia from New York, a state whose majority opposed the war, refused to cross the border and invade Canada. The men of the New York militia claimed they were not enlisted to serve outside New York State. He described their reaction: ". . . I rode in all directions, urging men by every consideration to pass, but in vain. . . ."[14] During this battle, Major General Sir Isaac Brock, a hero to the British and Canadians, was killed. His death devastated the men who had served under him.

On the Lake Champlain front in November, American general Henry Dearborn led his regular troops toward an attack on Montreal. The aging general, who was overweight and had difficulty

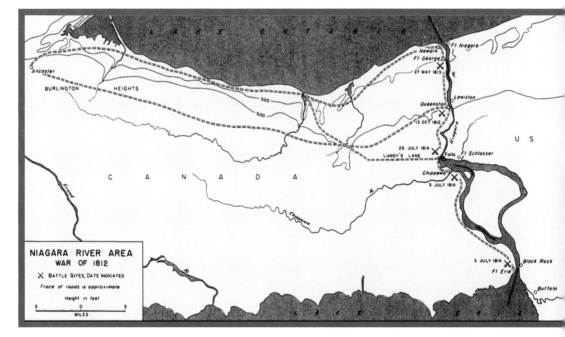

NIAGARA RIVER AREA
WAR OF 1812

✕ BATTLE SITES, DATE INDICATED
Trace of roads is approximate
Height in feet

△ This U.S. Army map shows the battles of the War of 1812 that took place in the Niagara River area.

moving around, did not inspire confidence in his troops, who nicknamed him "Granny." Dearborn had to abandon this plan because his militia also refused to cross into Canada to fight on foreign soil.

"Old Ironsides"

The United States forces did enjoy one surprising victory in 1812. It was the first major naval battle of the war, and it took place on August 19 off the coast of Maine. The USS *Constitution* was one of the finest warships in the American fleet. Swift and strong, it carried sixty cannons. The *Constitution,* commanded by Captain Isaac Hull, and the HMS *Guerrière,* a British frigate commanded by Captain James R. Dacres, fired cannonballs into each other. Shots bounced off the hull of the *Constitution,* earning it the nickname "Old Ironsides." In about fifteen minutes, the *Constitution* destroyed the *Guerrière.* This American success was repeated several more times during 1812, causing great embarrassment to Britain, whose navy was considered the most powerful in the world.

◁ *American victory at sea: The main and fore masts of the HMS* Guerrière *collapse under fire from the USS* Constitution *in this oil painting of the August 19, 1812, battle off the Maine coast.*

Major Campaigns of 1813

The second year of the war began with another tragedy for the United States: the slaughter of American soldiers in what became known as the River Raisin Massacre. On January 22, 1813, the British and Indians defeated General James Winchester and his militiamen, mostly Kentuckians. The battle took place at Frenchtown, on the frozen banks of the River Raisin, in what is now Michigan. The British left behind about thirty wounded Kentuckian prisoners of war. That night, American Indians massacred the helpless men. The American reaction was rage, and "Remember the River Raisin" became the new battle cry.

▲ *This British cartoon from 1813 celebrates the HMS* Shannon*'s victory over the USS* Chesapeake *on June 1 of that year. It casts the* Chesapeake*'s crew as cowardly while glorifying the* Shannon*'s boarding party, who triumphantly raise the British flag in victory.*

On April 27, 1813, American forces attacked York, now Toronto, which was the capital of Upper Canada. They ransacked homes and burned government buildings including the Parliament building, the seat of government. Penelope Beikie, a resident of York, wrote: "I kept my Castle, when all the rest fled, and it was well for us I did so,—our little property was saved by that means. Every house they found deserted was completely sacked."[15] It was an episode that the British would not forget. American troops held York for five days and then abandoned it, failing again to control Upper Canada.

Heroics at Sea

On June 1, 1813, the HMS *Shannon* challenged the USS *Chesapeake* to a one-on-one battle. The better-armed British vessel captured the *Chesapeake* and mortally wounded its captain, James Lawrence. As he lay dying, Lawrence commanded his men with the words "Do not give up the ship." Lawrence's words have since become the motto of the United States Navy.

American spirits soared when twenty-seven-year-old Commodore Oliver Perry led his tough little squadron and destroyed the British fleet on Lake Erie on September 10, 1813. During the battle, the British had severely damaged Perry's ship, but his men rowed him to another vessel, the *Niagara,* so that he could continue the fight. He reported his thrilling naval victory with these words: "We have met the enemy and they are ours." The result was that the United States controlled the Great Lakes.

▷ Death of Tecumseh

Perry's victory opened the way for General William Henry Harrison to invade Canada. On October 5, 1813, Harrison led another group of Kentucky militiamen against British Army troops and the Shawnee. The two sides met at the Thames River, north of Lake Erie. Wanting revenge, the Kentuckians shouted, "Remember the River Raisin!" Again, Harrison squared off against Tecumseh, the Shawnee chief. The battle

Oliver Hazard Perry, commanding the *Niagara,* led the American Navy to a crucial victory over a British squadron in the Battle of Lake Erie. Learn more about this naval hero and his military career on the **U.S. Brig *Niagara:* Oliver Hazard Perry** Web site.

ended fifty-five minutes later. Tecumseh was killed and with him died his dream of uniting American Indian nations into a confederation. The Battle of the Thames was a sound victory and a turning point because the United States gained control of most of the Northwest Territory.

1814—A New Phase of the War

As 1814 dawned, both sides strengthened their fighting forces. Britain, which had ended its war against France, was able to send fourteen thousand additional troops, supplies, and ships to fight in North America. The Royal Navy extended its blockade on the east coast of the United States to include New England. Merchant ships and naval vessels could not enter or leave American ports. Britain also planned a massive attack against the United States on three fronts: New York, Chesapeake Bay, and New Orleans.

In the United States, a new military leader emerged who improved the army. Winfield Scott was promoted to brigadier general at the young age of twenty-eight. A bold and energetic commander, Scott insisted that soldiers begin strict training with intense drills that lasted for ten hours a day. He also made sure that their camps were sanitary so that the troops could remain healthy. He enforced discipline in dress and in conduct to such an extent that he came to be referred to as "Old Fuss and Feathers." Soldiers and officers gained new respect for themselves, and morale improved. The United States Army grew stronger and better prepared to wage war.

Horseshoe Bend

The first major battle in 1814 came on March 27 at Horseshoe Bend in what is today Alabama. This area of mostly forested land got its name from the Tallapoosa River "curling back" on itself to form a peninsula. A year earlier, the United States government, intent on taking Indian lands so that white Americans could settle on them, had begun a war with the American Indian people it called the Creek. Now it wanted to crush the Creek Nation once and for all. Andrew Jackson, a major general of the Tennessee Militia, was the feisty general who planned the attack. His force of thirty-two hundred consisted mainly of white Americans, but it also included six hundred "friendly" Cherokee and Creek warriors. Jackson and his men stormed the village that the Creek had built at Horseshoe Bend. Almost one thousand Creek men, women, and children lost their lives. It was an overwhelming victory for Jackson and the United States and a devastating defeat for the Creek, who signed a peace treaty that turned over 20 million acres of their ancient lands in Georgia and Alabama to the United States.

Before the British could attack the United States again, American forces invaded Canada once more, and this time they succeeded. They crossed the Niagara River and defeated the British at Chippewa,

The Madison Era: Native Americans: Tecumseh: Battle of Thames - Microsoft Internet Explorer

File Edit View Favorites Tools Help

Address http://www.jmu.edu/madison/center/main_pages/madison_archives/era/native/tecumseh/image3.htm

Information

Teacher Resources

Montpelier

Additional Material

Search

Contact Us

A biography of Tecumseh (whose death is dramatized in this print), a letter he wrote to William Henry Harrison, and accounts of his death at the Battle of the Thames can be found at **The James Madison Center—Tecumseh: An American Hero.**

near Niagara Falls, on July 5. The troops continued along the river to their next battle, three miles away at Lundy's Lane.

▷ Lundy's Lane

The Battle of Lundy's Lane, fought on July 25, was one of the bloodiest battles of the war. For that reason it has been called the Gettysburg of Canada, a reference to the pivotal battle in the American Civil War. On a hot summer night near Niagara Falls, American soldiers collided with British and Canadian soldiers. The two armies clashed in a confusing battle, amid darkness and smoke, unable to recognize friend or enemy. They fought to the point of exhaustion. By morning, more than one third of the combatants were killed.

After the battle, both sides claimed victory. United States major general Jacob Brown declared that ". . . the enemy . . . were driven from every position they attempted to hold . . . notwithstanding his immense superiority both in numbers and position, he was completely defeated. . . ."[16] British lieutenant general Gordon Drummond reported that the day had ". . . been crowned with complete success by the defeat of the enemy and his retreat to the position of Chippawa. . . ."[17] The American Army withdrew to Fort Erie, where it defeated British and Canadian forces and then crossed back into the United States. This was the last attempt by the United States to invade its neighbor to the north.

Britain Strikes Back

The British launched their three-pronged invasion of the United States in August by moving up Chesapeake Bay and attacking Washington City and Baltimore. British frigates, carrying four thousand

Wisconsin Historical Society: The War of 1812

Access this Web site from http://www.myreportlinks.com

This Web site from the Wisconsin Historical Society provides a brief overview of Wisconsin's role in the War of 1812. Primary documents from the society's collections are also included.

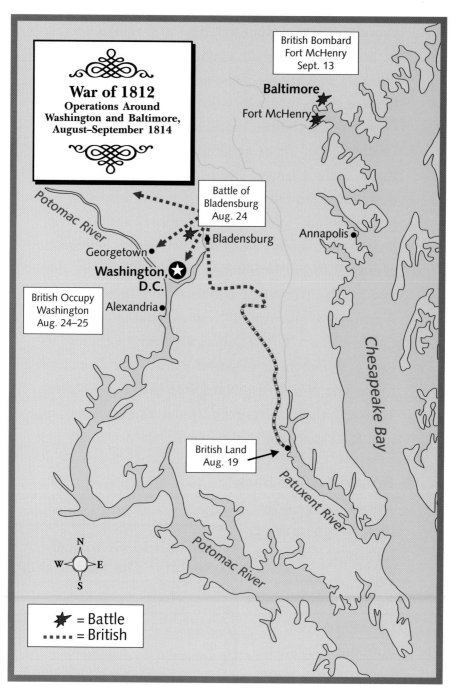

War of 1812
Operations Around
Washington and Baltimore,
August–September 1814

British Bombard
Fort McHenry
Sept. 13

Baltimore

Fort McHenry

Battle of
Bladensburg
Aug. 24

Bladensburg

Annapolis

Georgetown

Washington,
D.C.

British Occupy
Washington
Aug. 24–25

Alexandria

Potomac River

Chesapeake Bay

British Land
Aug. 19

Patuxent River

Potomac River

N
W E
S

★ = Battle
••••• = British

This map tracks the military operations around Baltimore, Maryland, and Washington, D.C., from August through September 1814.

troops, sailed up the Potomac and Patuxent rivers. The British brought the war to Washington City, where they torched government buildings. They caused millions of dollars in damage and, most importantly to their cause, humiliated the American people.

"The Rocket's Red Glare"

Baltimore was next. This city, with its fine harbor, was an attractive target because it was a wealthy seaport and a home port for American privateers. As British soldiers marched to the city, warships from the Royal Navy took aim at Fort McHenry, which guarded the harbor. Along the way, British general Robert Ross was shot and killed. The residents were expecting an attack and had strengthened Fort McHenry. At 6:30 A.M. on September 13, British warships began to bombard the fort. They hurled Congreve rockets that lit up the night sky and exploded with a deafening roar. These twenty-pound rockets, named for their designer, English artillery expert William Congreve, could travel up to two miles, a vast improvement over earlier rockets. Cannonballs were exchanged between the fort and the warships and continued furiously until 7:00 the next morning. The Americans' defense of Fort McHenry was a success. The British fleet and army retreated. The star-spangled banner was raised over the fort, inspiring a young Washington attorney, Francis Scott Key, to write the words that would become the lyrics for the national anthem. The failed attack on Fort McHenry helped persuade Britain to consider ending the war.

In September, the British continued their invasion by marching into northern New York State. Led by General Sir George Prevost, fifteen thousand British troops traveled south from Canada and occupied the town of Plattsburg, on the western bank of Lake Champlain. To protect its army, the Royal Navy sailed into Plattsburg Bay and, on September 11, British ships fired on American ships anchored there. Commodore Thomas MacDonough commanded the

The Mariners' Museum : Birth of the U.S. Navy - Microsoft Internet Explorer

File Edit View Favorites Tools Help

Address http://www.mariner.org/usnavy/caption_pages/09q_LE2060MacDonough.htm

THOMAS MACDONOUGH, U.S.N.

Commodore Thomas MacDonough, commanding a much smaller American fleet, staged a stunning defeat of the British at Plattsburg. Learn more about MacDonough at **The Mariners' Museum: The Naval War of 1812** Web site.

smaller American fleet. The fighting raged for two hours and twenty minutes and ended when General Prevost ordered the entire British fleet to surrender. This was a stunning victory for MacDonough and made him a naval legend. Even though he was out-gunned, his well-planned strategy overpowered the British fleet. In *The Naval War of 1812,* written by a twenty-three-year-old student named Theodore Roosevelt, who would go on to become the United States president from 1901 to 1909, Roosevelt praised the naval officer:

Macdonough in this battle won a higher fame than any other commander of the war, British or American. . . . it was solely owing to his foresight and resource that we won the victory. . . . Down to the time of the Civil War he is the greatest figure in our naval history. [18]

Roosevelt summed up the battle:

The effects of the victory were immediate and of the highest importance. Sir George Prevost and his army at once fled in great haste and confusion back to Canada, leaving our northern frontier clear for the remainder of the war; while the victory had a very great effect on the negotiations for peace. [19]

The crushing defeat at Plattsburg convinced the British government to put an end to this costly war.

▶ 1814: A Final Battle and Peace

The Battle of New Orleans was the final part of the British plan to invade the United States. But this last and most famous battle of the War of 1812 actually took place fifteen days after a peace treaty had been signed. Neither side's forces knew about the treaty when they went into battle because slow communications prevented word of the treaty reaching the United States in time.

The British wanted to control New Orleans because of its important location at the entrance to the Mississippi River. On the morning of January 8, General Sir Edward Pakenham led fifty-three hundred British soldiers on a march to attack the city. General Andrew Jackson had secured New Orleans for the assault. He led a group of forty-five hundred men that included regular army troops, militia, Choctaw Indians in war paint, Kentucky sharpshooters, Tennessee frontiersmen carrying knives and tomahawks, and a band of outlaws led by the pirate Jean Laffite. General Jackson needed more recruits, so he issued a special proclamation "To the Free Colored Inhabitants of Louisiana," saying that it was a mistake that African Americans were

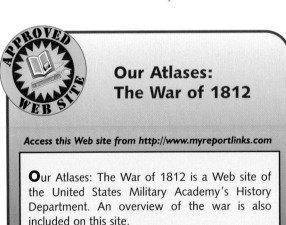

**Our Atlases:
The War of 1812**

Access this Web site from http://www.myreportlinks.com

Our Atlases: The War of 1812 is a Web site of the United States Military Academy's History Department. An overview of the war is also included on this site.

not allowed to enlist. He urged them to volunteer, promising they ". . . will be paid the same bounty in money and lands now received by white soldiers of the United States. . . ."[20]

The Battle of New Orleans lasted less than two hours, and the British retreated. The cost in human lives was two thousand British killed and only eight Americans killed. The stunning victory made Jackson a national hero, helping him later to be elected president. January 8 became a national holiday, with celebrations and parades. The anniversary of the battle is still celebrated in New Orleans and Nashville.

The Treaty of Ghent

Even before the war's end, British and American diplomats began discussing plans for peace. In August 1814, British and American representatives met in the city of Ghent, in Belgium, to negotiate the terms. The Treaty of Ghent was signed on Christmas Eve 1814, two weeks before the Battle of New Orleans. Again, as with the beginning of war, slow communication was a problem. Word of the treaty did not reach the United States in time to prevent the final battle.

Chapter 3

IN THEIR OWN WORDS: AMERICAN SOLDIERS AND SAILORS

Some of the men who served in the United States Army and Navy during the War of 1812 kept journals and diaries of their experiences. They wrote letters home to friends and loved ones when there was a break in the fighting. Such accounts give us an idea of the personal feelings of those in combat and offer a glimpse of what daily life was like for them. These letters and journals show us the human side of war.

▷ Battlefield Stories: Soldiers

In the early campaigns of the war, the United States Army lacked adequate food and supplies. In the

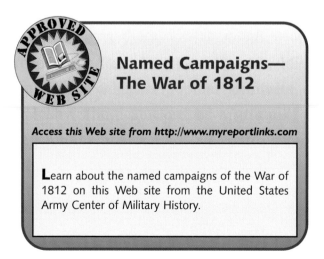

Named Campaigns— The War of 1812

Access this Web site from http://www.myreportlinks.com

Learn about the named campaigns of the War of 1812 on this Web site from the United States Army Center of Military History.

winter of 1812, soldiers were suffering from the frigid temperatures and hunger. Brigadier General James Winchester's troops, stationed near Fort Dearborn, on Lake Michigan, survived on rotten beef, pork, and hickory nuts. On Christmas Eve, one soldier wrote,

Our sufferings in this place have been greater than if we had been in severe battle. More than one hundred lives have been lost, owing to the bad accommodations. The sufferings of about three hundred sick at a time, who are exposed to the cold ground and deprived of every nourishment, are sufficient proof of our wretched condition.[1]

Conditions in the battlefield hospitals were awful. Dr. William Beaumont, an American surgeon's mate, or assistant, treated three hundred wounded soldiers from both sides during the Battle of York in April 1813. Dr. Beaumont recorded the sounds and sights of the battlefield where, "wading in blood," he operated on fifty patients in two days.

Their wounds were of the worst kind, compd [compound] fractures of *legs, thighs, & arms* and fractures of *Sculls*. . . . I cut and slashed for 48 hours, without food or sleep—My God! who can think of the shocking scene, where his fellow creatures lye mashed & mangled in evry part with a leg—an Arm—a head, or a body ground in pieces.[2]

"Into Battle We Must Go"

Jarvis Hanks was not yet fourteen years old when he enlisted as a drummer in the United States Army. He came from a village in Vermont. Hanks was paid the sum of $20 in advance and 160 acres of land for his service. He was assigned to the Eleventh United States Infantry, and before long he witnessed the grim side of military life.

Hanks later wrote vivid accounts of his wartime dangers and hardships. He endured twenty-six months in the army ". . . often weary and exhausted with marches for weeks together; sometimes being so hungry and to be willing, eagerly to devour turnip peelings floating in dirty water of a ferry boat; and on one occasion to eat what was decided to be 'horse beef.'"[3] On marching into battle at Lundy's Lane

In his letter of March 30, 1815, C. Blake, a lieutenant in the Ninth U.S. Infantry, tells his brother William that he is "yet alive" following the bloody and hard-fought battle at Lundy's Lane.

with his drum slung over his shoulder, young Hanks wrote about the dangers of being a drummer.

Musicians are placed in the rear of the colors, in the center of the regiment or battalion, and as the aim of enemies respectively is mainly to shoot down the flags, and as the falling or striking of a flag is a signal of surrender; it seems to me that musicians thus situated are in equal danger with any other portion of the army. I remember, a trumpeter was riding back, furiously, wounded, with the blood streaming, profusely down his temples & cheeks. As I was also a musician, I felt much alarmed for my own safety, not knowing but I should be in as bad or a worse situation in a few minutes. There was no stopping, nor escape, into battle we must go.[4]

▷ Battlefield Stories: Militiamen

Most of the wounded American soldiers massacred at the River Raisin in January 1813 were Kentucky militiamen. James C. Price was a captain who led the Kentuckians. A few days before the battle began, Captain Price wrote to his wife, Susan, about how their only son should be raised should he, the boy's father, not survive:

In Camp, near raisin River, Jan. 16, 1813.
Dear Susan:

I have only time to inform you that we expect to have a battle tomorrow with the British and Indians. On the eve of battle I have believed it proper to address you these lines. . . . My only son, I feel a great interest in his future life and welfare. . . . Teach my boy to love truth, to speak truth at all times. He must not be allowed to associate with children or other persons who indulge in swearing or misrepresentations [lies]. He must be taught to bear in mind that "an honest man" is the "noblest work of God"; he must be rigidly honest in his dealings. . . . Not a day must be lost in teaching him how to work, and the great principles of our holy religion must be on all occasions impressed on his mind. It may be possible I may fall in battle and my only boy must know that his father, next to God, loves his country, and is now risking his life in defending that country against a barbarous and cruel enemy.[5]

Sadly, Captain Price did not survive the battle. Acting Captain William Caldwell wrote to Price's mother: "You will, long before this reaches you, have received the painful intelligence of the death of your brave and gallant son, Capt. James C. Price, who was

▲ This 1871 photograph includes veterans of the War of 1812 who survived the River Raisin Massacre. Joseph Guyor (middle row, far right) invited fellow veterans to gather at his house for a "free dance and reunion." Refreshments were served by veterans of the "late war," the Civil War. One of those was George Armstrong Custer (top row, third from left).

killed and scalped by the Indians on the morning of January 22d."[6]

Another soldier, A. G. Tustin, wrote to his mother on January 23, 1813, describing the massacre:

> Never, dear mother, if I should live a thousand years, can I forget the frightful sight of this morning, when handsomely painted Indians came into the fort, some of them carrying half a dozen scalps of my countrymen fastened upon sticks, and yet covered with blood, and were congratulated by (British) Colonel Proctor for their *bravery*.[7]

Away at battle for months, soldiers worried about plantings, crops, harvests, and their families left back home without money. John Hollyday, a soldier from Ohio, wrote to May, his wife: "Affectionate Companion . . . It gives me a great deal of satisfaction to hear that the corn is planted and that you expect it will be tended for I did not look for that to be done." A few weeks later, he wrote about his service in the army: "The men is grumbling that they have to work so hard and is not like to get any pay but for my part I dont care about the pay I want to put in my touer of duty and go home to my family money is not my object but to serve my time and come home with honor."[8]

▶ Naval Stories: Sailors

At the outbreak of war, the United States Navy was ill prepared to fight, especially against the Royal

The uniforms of some United States Army officers and enlisted men at the time of the War of 1812. A captain of infantry stands in front of enlisted infantrymen. On horseback are a major general and a brigadier general.

Navy. In 1812, the United States Navy had fewer than twenty seagoing ships, few trained sailors, and not enough supplies. Master Commandant Charles Ludlow worried because his sailors lacked warm clothing for the freezing winter months. In November 1812, he wrote to Secretary of the Navy Paul Hamilton. For each sailor, he requested ". . . one Mattress, two blankets, 1 pr of shoes & stockings and a suit of thick Cloaths. . . ."[9]

When the HMS *Shannon* seized the USS *Chesapeake* in June 1813, a midshipman named William Berry was hiding from the British. Here is Berry's account of his capture:

> Lieutenant Faulkner (the British officer) said to his men, kill those damned rascals. Then, and immediately, several muskets were discharged at them, but without effect. . . . Lieutenant Faulkner looked up in the mizen-top [top of a mast]; pointed at me,—said to his men, go up, three of you, and throw that damned yankee overboard. They immediately rushed up, seizing me by the collar; now, said they, you damned yankee, you shall swim for it, attempting to throw me overboard; but I got within the rigging, when one of them kicked me in the breast, which was the cause of my falling; being stunned by the fall, I lay some time senseless, and when I came to, I was cut over the head with a cutlass. . . .[10]

Dr. Usher Parsons was a twenty-five-year-old surgeon with the Lake Erie Squadron. He was the only surgeon available for duty when Oliver Perry won his great victory on Lake Erie. In a letter to his parents, Parsons described the circumstances under which he treated about one hundred sick and wounded men: "Dear Parents, . . . I had some narrow escapes for my life during the action, five cannon balls passed through the room in which I was attending to the wounded. . . ."[11]

After Commodore Stephen Decatur captured a British frigate, he wrote a romantic letter to his wife:

My Beloved Susan,
I have gained a small sprig of laurel, which I shall hasten to lay at your feet . . . but now that I have a precious little wife, I wish to have something more substantial to offer in case she should become weary of love and glory . . . Do not be anxious about me, my beloved, I shall soon press you to my heart.[12]

▶ Naval Stories: American Privateersmen

The United States depended on privateers to help fight the war on the seas. A typical privateer was a well-designed, fast-sailing vessel that could outrun the British warships. By bringing in captured British ships, the privateers' owners and crews earned bounties that amounted to thousands of dollars.

Newspapers printed details of captures and listed the cargo that was seized. The best-known privateer was the *Prince de Neufchatel*. On its first cruise, it sailed into the English Channel and captured six British vessels. It was chased seventeen times during

▲ *An American privateer, the* General Armstrong, *is pictured. These fast-sailing vessels helped fight the war on the seas during the War of 1812.*

the summer of 1814 but managed to escape the enemy every time. The cargo it captured and brought safely into port in 1814 sold for almost $3 million. According to the *Niles Weekly Register,* after one encounter, the *Prince* hauled in ". . . 140 bales, 164 boxes and 156 trunks of dry goods, 23 casks and 174 boxes sweet oil, and a large quantity of coffee, rum and various other articles, and 20 prisoners. She [the ship] arrived at Boston, October 15."[13]

Prisoners of War: Tales of Despair From Dartmoor

Great Britain used prison ships and jails throughout its empire to hold American prisoners of war. The worst was Dartmoor, in southwestern England, used for prisoners captured on the high seas. Prison officials often abused the prisoners, who suffered from cold, damp conditions and lack of food. Stories of the horrors endured by the American prisoners held there did not become known until after the war ended, when some of them wrote about their experiences.

Perez Drinkwater was on a privateer when he was captured, shipped to England, and marched to Dartmoor in a snowstorm. In a letter to his wife, Sally, he described the conditions:

> This same place is one of the most retched in this habbited world . . . neither wind nor water tight, it is situated on the top of a high hill and is so high that it either rains, hails or snows almost the year round. . . . So I must conclude with telling you that I am not alone for there is almost 5,000 of us heir [here], and creepers [insects] a 1000 to one.[14]

Benjamin Waterhouse, a surgeon who was captured and shipped to England, had this to say about his treatment at Dartmoor: "After we had finished our own dinners in New England, we give to our cats and dogs more solid nourishment, the remnant

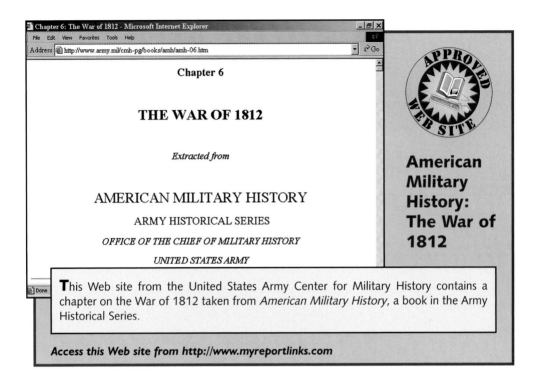

Chapter 6: The War of 1812 - Microsoft Internet Explorer

File   Edit   View   Favorites   Tools   Help

Address http://www.army.mil/cmh-pg/books/amh/amh-06.htm   Go

Chapter 6

THE WAR OF 1812

Extracted from

AMERICAN MILITARY HISTORY

ARMY HISTORICAL SERIES

OFFICE OF THE CHIEF OF MILITARY HISTORY

UNITED STATES ARMY

Done

American Military History: The War of 1812

This Web site from the United States Army Center for Military History contains a chapter on the War of 1812 taken from *American Military History,* a book in the Army Historical Series.

Access this Web site from http://www.myreportlinks.com

of our meals, than what we had often allowed us in the ships and prisons."[15] Another American prisoner in Dartmoor had this observation: ". . . an American, in England, pines to get home; while an Englishman . . . longs to become an American citizen."[16]

Mounting tensions at the prison exploded on the night of April 6, 1815, resulting in the Dartmoor Massacre. British guards fired on the inmates, killing seven and wounding thirty-one. Nathaniel Pierce, an imprisoned seaman, witnessed the massacre: "I can compare it to nothing but firing into a hencoup among a parcel of fowls."[17] The prisoners were released at the end of April 1815.

AMERICAN INDIAN, BRITISH, AND CANADIAN STORIES

When the War of 1812 began, the British Army stationed in Canada did not fight alone. Their allies included American Indians and Canadian militiamen. All of these were supported by the men of the Royal Navy, the undisputed superpower of the seas. Like their American counterparts, British and Canadian soldiers and sailors wrote letters to family and friends and kept journals of their adventures on land and water. Their stories capture the drama of the war that, to the British, would come to be known as the Anglo-American War.

▶ A Native American Account

The War of 1812 was fought by specific rules of warfare. Some historians called it a gentlemen's war because opposing sides met for discussions, exchanged letters, and even offered hospitality.

◀ *Black Hawk, a chief of the Sauk and Fox, fought alongside Tecumseh in the War of 1812. Unlike Tecumseh, Black Hawk survived to lead his people in a war against western settlement in the 1830s.*

Black Hawk, chief of the Sauk and Fox nations, thought it absurd the way the British and Americans fought. This is his description of the white man's method of combat:

> Instead of stealing upon each other and taking every advantage to *kill the enemy* and *save our own people,* as we do (which, with us, is considered good policy in a war chief), they march out, in open daylight, and fight regardless of the number of warriors they may lose.
>
> After the battle is over, they retire to feast and drink wine, as if nothing had happened; after which, they make a *statement in writing* of what they have done—*each party claiming the victory!* and neither giving an account of half the number that have been killed on their own side. They all fought like braves, but would not do to *lead a war party* with us.[1]

▷ Battlefield Stories: A British Private in Canada

Life was harsh for British regulars in Canada. Serving thousands of miles away from home across the ocean, they had to adjust to living and fighting in a freezing climate in a strange, uncharted wilderness.

A British private named Shadrach Byfield kept an account of his service in Canada. Born in England, Byfield enlisted in the British Army and was sent to Canada where he served for twenty-six months. There were one hundred ten members in his company when he arrived. Two years later, only Byfield and fourteen others were still alive. His narrative shows a young man who was as tough as nails.

Byfield helped collect prisoners at the Battle of Detroit. He wrote, "Whilst walking along, I slipped and nearly fell, one of the men said, 'My dear man, that is the brains of a man killed with one of your shots.'"[2]

During war, soldiers think about death. Byfield had a close call during the battle at the River Raisin. His account probably echoes the sentiments of other soldiers:

It being now light, I saw a man come from the fence when I said to my comrade, "There is a man, I'll have a shot at him." Just as I said these words and pulled my trigger, I received a ball under my left ear and fell immediately; in falling I cut my comrade's leg with my bayonet. He exclaimed, "Byfield is dead." To which I

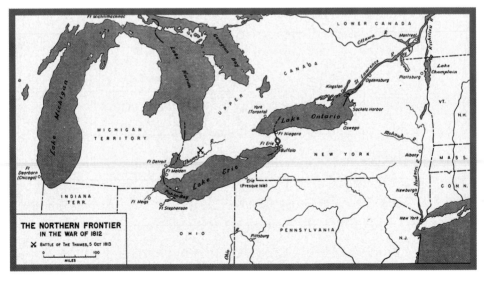

▲ The northern frontier in the War of 1812 is the subject of this U.S. Army map, which pinpoints the site of the Battle of the Thames.

replied, "I believe I be," and I thought to myself, is this death, or how men do die? As soon as I had recovered so as to raise my head from the ground, I crept away upon my hands and knees.[3]

Byfield luckily survived fighting on the front lines in a number of fierce battles. But after he was wounded again in August 1814, the twenty-five-year-old was sent back to England.

▶ Battlefield Stories: A British Officer in Canada

A young British officer, John LeCouteur, was an eighteen-year-old lieutenant in the 104th Foot, a regiment stationed in Upper Canada. He kept a lengthy record detailing the hardships he endured: illness, storms, food shortages, heroic marches, skirmishes, and major battles.

LeCouteur described a seven-hundred-mile march he and his regiment made in the dead of winter:

When we got to the end of our day's march the cold was so intense that the men could scarcely use their fingers to hew down the fire-wood, or to build huts. . . . On the morning of the 5th [of March 1813] the cold had greatly augmented and the thermometer once more fell to 27 degrees below zero, together with a gale, a north-wester in our teeth, which scarcely left us power to breathe. . . .[4]

During the war, there were moments of kindness shown to wounded enemy soldiers. LeCouteur fought in the Battle of Lundy's Lane. His entry for Monday, July 25, 1814, the day of the battle, included this account.

There were three hundred dead on the Niagara side of the hillock, and about a hundred of ours, besides several hundred wounded. The miserable badly-wounded were groaning and imploring us for water, the Indians prowling about them and scalping or plundering. Close by me lay a fine young man, the son of the American general Hull. He was mortally wounded, and I gave him some brandy and water. . . . He told me much about Himself and to come to Him in the morning. . . . When I got to Him, He was a beautiful Corpse. . . . [5]

▶ Battlefield Stories: Canadian Militiamen

Physically fit Canadian males between the ages of sixteen and sixty were required to serve in a local militia. At the time of the war, there were about sixty thousand in Lower Canada and about eleven thousand in Upper Canada.[6] The militia were generally untrained and in desperate need of supplies. They were responsible for transporting supplies, building roads and fortifications, and guarding prisoners. Some well-trained militia units fought with the British regulars.

Jacques Viger was a captain in the Lower Canada militia. He kept a diary during his service in the war in the summer of 1813. Viger joined the garrison at Kingston, where he complained about camp life.

We now occupy tents which we again once more put up in a wilderness of stumps, fallen trees, boulders, and rocks of all sizes and shapes; sharing our blanket with reptiles of varied species; . . . ten million insects and crawling abominations, the ones more voracious and disgusting than the others. . . . Pray for us! Pray for us! ye pious souls.[7]

There were serious shortages of food and clothing because supplies were often stolen by allies or by the enemy. Colonel Joel Stone made this request of his superior: "I have furnished barracks for one hundred and twenty men. . . . And all are in the greatest want of almost every necessary . . . stoves, blankets, etc. and I must observe that we are in as great want of shoes, pantaloons [pants], jackets, and watch coats for the Guard."[8]

Thomas G. Ridout, a lieutenant of the Upper Canada militia, wrote about military hardships. He complained about food shortages in a letter to his father:

Tonight our dragoon (cavalry) is to make a grand attack on the onions. The nests are kept very nice and clean from eggs. The dragoon has just come in with a fine musk melon and a peck of onions. We feed a turkey at the door, which is doomed for our Sunday dinner. [9]

Ridout also wrote to his brother George: ". . . I carry on an extensive robbery of pears, apples, onions, corn, carrots [etc.] for we can get nothing but by stealing excepting some milk, which by the by is carefully measured. Bread and butter is out of the question. . . . "[10]

Because of the shortages, desertion was a major problem for both sides. A soldier's life was not a healthy one. Disease took the lives of more soldiers in the war than battle wounds. Poor hygiene, lack of food and clothing, and rampant disease all took a toll on the troops. Thomas Ridout reported to his

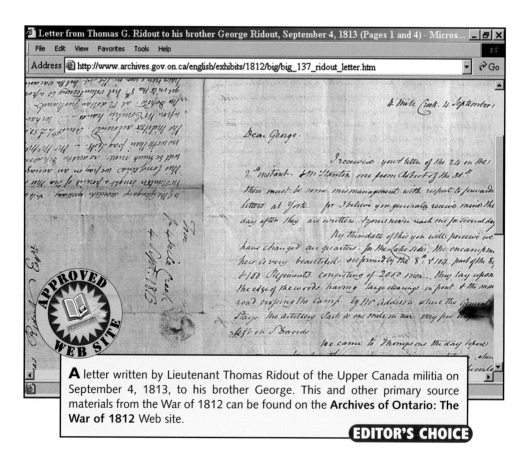

Letter from Thomas G. Ridout to his brother George Ridout, September 4, 1813 (Pages 1 and 4) - Micros...

File   Edit   View   Favorites   Tools   Help

Address   http://www.archives.gov.on.ca/english/exhibits/1812/big/big_137_ridout_letter.htm   Go

A letter written by Lieutenant Thomas Ridout of the Upper Canada militia on September 4, 1813, to his brother George. This and other primary source materials from the War of 1812 can be found on the **Archives of Ontario: The War of 1812** Web site.

EDITOR'S CHOICE

brother George in a letter, "Desertion has come to such height that 8 or 10 men go off daily. . . ."[11]

William McCay was a lieutenant colonel in the Upper Canada militia. He and his regiment were ready to storm Fort Detroit. McCay's diary entries for a few days in August 1812 tell of General Hull's surrender and Americans taken as prisoners of war.

August 16: . . . the American flag came down while the British was hoisted amid the shouts of the whole Army. . . . There were between 2500 and 3000 made prisoners of war. . . . The [American] regulars . . . were . . . dirty and ragged, owing, they told us, to their marching a great distance, through a wilderness, and not receiving their pay or clothing. I never saw such a day in my life. . . .[12]

Stories From the Royal Navy

By 1814, Britain wanted stronger naval operations along the Atlantic coast. The day after Vice Admiral Sir Alexander Cochrane took up command of the North American station in 1814, he issued a proclamation inviting African slaves to join British forces. It said that those who wished to leave the United States ". . . will have their choice of either entering into His Majesty's sea or land forces, or of being sent as FREE settlers to the British possessions in North America or the West Indies, where they will meet with all due encouragement."[13] Eventually about

**Archives of Ontario:
The War of 1812**

Access this Web site from http://www.myreportlinks.com

Letters from British captain William Merritt to the American woman he fell in love with can also be found on the Archives of Ontario: The War of 1812 Web site.

EDITOR'S CHOICE

four thousand slaves left their owners.[14] Almost three hundred slaves served with the British in the Chesapeake Bay area.[15]

Edward Codrington, a British captain, blamed the naval defeats on inexperienced crews and excessively harsh discipline. In a letter to his wife, Codrington complained that there was too much favoritism in the British service and that American officers performed better because they were chosen on merit. He stated that this was the case even on former "crack ships," where "the people, from being tyrannically treated, would rejoice in being captured by the Americans, from whom they would receive every encouragement."[16]

Seaman Samuel Leech served aboard the HMS *Macedonian* until it was captured by the USS *United States* in October 1812. His account of the battle described the heartfelt grief of one of his shipmates who saw his friend die.

It was really a touching spectacle to see the rough, hardy features of the brave old sailor streaming with tears, as he picked out the dead body of his friend from among the wounded and gently carried it to the ship's side, saying . . . "O Bill, we have sailed together in a number of ships, we have been in many gales and

some battles, but this is the worst day I have seen!
We must now part!" Here he dropped the body into
the deep, and . . . added, "I can do no more for you.
Farewell! God be with you!"[17]

▷ A Prisoner in Love

British soldiers and seamen who were captured by
the United States were either exchanged or sent to
prisons. Officers and regular troops were treated as
gentlemen. William Hamilton Merritt was a British
captain captured by the Americans at the Battle of
Lundy's Lane in 1814. Before the war, Merritt had
met and fallen in love with Catherine Prendergast,
an American living in New York. In September 1812,
the captain wrote to his fiancée:

> The unhappy situation which our Countries are placed
> in will deprive me [from] time of the greatest pleasure
> I have ever enjoyed viz. [namely] seeing you, . . . if I
> should be separated from you for years I will ever
> remain the same as you left me.[18]

When the war ended, Merritt returned to
Canada, and Catherine Prendergast followed him.
They were married in 1815.

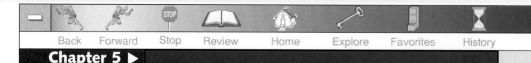
IN THE WORDS
OF CIVILIANS

Many civilians also kept journals and diaries and wrote memoirs that told how their lives were affected by the war. These civilians included families of the soldiers and sailors as well as regular townspeople who lived in areas where the fighting took place. Their accounts provide valuable insight into the world in which they lived. They are not to be read as accurate military descriptions of countries at war. They come with personal prejudices and biases, but they recount often-colorful episodes of the war from an ordinary citizen's point of view.

▶ Letters and Diaries of American Civilians

Women were not allowed to fight in the war. A few had permission to accompany their husbands to their military assignments where they cooked, sewed, and helped as nurses. Lydia Bacon was the wife of a soldier in the 4th Infantry and moved with him from camp to camp. On her way to Detroit, she was captured and made a prisoner ". . . to His Majesty King George 3d. . . ." She wrote about her treatment by a British lieutenant who ". . . observing we were Officers Wives, he assured us we should be treated as such, politely invited us to his Quarters till we procured a room at the Public House. . . ." Mrs. Bacon was then ". . . introduced to his wife, a very pleasant lady, & their only Child, a Babe in her Arms, Cake & c [coffee] was offered us, & for a time we almost forgot our real situation."[1]

When she was released, Mrs. Bacon made her way to Detroit, which she described as ". . . a beautiful part of our Country, good gardens in the Village, & fine farms in the vicinity, had a delightful ride horseback on the bank of the river above Detroit."[2]

Mrs. Bacon was inside Fort Detroit on August 16, 1812, when it was bombarded by the British, and General Hull surrendered. She recorded what she saw:

> . . . the enemys shot began to enter the Fort, & as some Ladies were making cylinders (bags to hold the powder), & scraping lint in case it should be wanted, a 24 pound shot entered the next door . . . and cut two Officers who were standing in the entry directly in two their bowels gushing out, the same ball passed through the Wall into a room where a number of people were & took the legs of one man off & the flesh of the thigh of another . . . never shall I forget my sensation as I crossed the Parade ground to gain the place of safty. . . .[3]

Margaret St. John lived in Buffalo, New York, when the British landed and attacked in December 1813. The alarmed townspeople fled, blocking every road that led from the city. Mrs. St. John was left behind at her home with two of her daughters. An account of her bravery was written by her daughter Martha.

My mother said she saw an Indian pulling the curtains down from the window of the Lovejoy house opposite, and saw Mrs. Lovejoy strike his hand with a carving-knife, and saw the Indian raise the hatchet; but as the door closed she could not know certain that he killed her. She did not dare to go and see.

Soon there came . . . a British colonel on horseback. He spoke very cross, and said: "Why are you not away?" Mother said she had lost the opportunity now she had nowhere to go to, only out in and perish in the snow. He said: "I have just seen a very unpleasant sight in the house over the way. The Indians have killed a woman, and I am very sorry any such thing should happen." "Well," said mother, "I was fearful she would provoke them to kill her." I spoke to her and said: "Do not risk your life for property"; she answered: "When my property goes, my life shall go with it."[4]

CAMP at DETROIT 16 August 1812.

CAPITULATION for the Surrender of Fort DETROIT, entered into between Major General BROCK, commanding His BRITANNIC MAJESTY's forces, on the one part; & Brigadier General HULL, commanding the North-Weſtern Army of the UNITED-STATES on the other part.

1ſt. Fort DETROIT, with all the troops, regulars as well as Militia, will be immediately Surrendered to the Britiſh forces under the Command of Maj. Gen. BROCK, & will be conſidered priſoners of war, with the exception of ſuch of the Militia of the MICHIGAN Territory who have not joined the Army.

2d. All public Stores, arms & all public documents including every thing elſe of a public nature will be immediately given up.

3d. Private Perſons & property of every deſcription ſhall be reſpected.

4th. His excellency Brigadier Gen. HULL having expreſſed a deſire that a detachment from the State of Ohio, on its way to join his Army, as well as one ſent from Fort DETROIT, under the Command of Colonel Mc ARTHUR, ſhould be included in the above CAPITULATION, it is accordingly agreed to. It is however to be underſtood that ſuch part of the Ohio - Militia, as have not joined the Army, will be permitted to return to their homes, on condition that they will not ſerve during the war; their arms however will be delivered up, if belonging to the public.

5th. The Garriſon will march out at the hour of twelve o'clock, & the British forces will take immediately poſſeſſion of the Fort.

APPROVED,
(SIGNED) W. HULL, Brigr. Genl. Comg. the N.W. Army.
APPROVED.
(SIGNED) ISAAC BROCK, Major General.

(Signed.) J. Mc. DONELL Lieut. Col. Militia. P. A. D. C.
J. B. GLEGG Major A. D- C.
JAMES MILLER Lieut. Col. 5th. U. S. Infantry.
E. BRUSH Col. Comg. 1ſt .Regtt Michigan Militia.

A true Copy.

ROBERT NICHOL Lieut. Colt & Qr. M. Genl. Militia.

The terms of the surrender of Fort Detroit by Brigadier General William Hull to Major General Isaac Brock. The American surrender was viewed as a national disgrace.

Mrs. St. John went to British general Phineas Riall and begged that her houses not be burned down. Riall agreed, but her larger house was burned by Indians anyway.

▷ Abducted

The following is an account by Joshua Penny, who was abducted by the British during the middle of the night while he, his wife, and three children slept. Penny earlier had tried to torpedo a British ship in Long Island Harbor, but failed. An informer told the British where he lived, and during the night of August 20, 1813, they went knocking on his door:

"Mr. Penny, we want you to get up immediately." I . . . sprang out of my bed, and in my shirt ran for my gun. . . . They saw me through the window as I opened the kitchen door . . . When they perceived me aiming for the gun, they burst in the door, and surrounded me. . . . They took me . . . to lieut. Lawrence. . . . He presented a pistol to my nose, and attempted to shoot me. I never saw more fire issue from a lock in my life—it flew into my eyes—it rolled on the floor; but as luck would have it, missed fire! . . . My wife followed us to the door and shrieked; upon which a sergeant of marines struck her with the breech of a gun. . . .

I spoke with the lieutenant—"Sir, you are not surely going to burn my wife and children!" It appeared they had come prepared to burn the house, but were afraid of the militia; and thus hurried off. [5]

Penny was taken to Melville Island Prison, in Halifax, Nova Scotia, and released nine months later.

▷ A Missing Husband

Mrs. Jane Stinger wrote an unusual letter to Secretary of the Navy Paul Hamilton, asking that her husband be dismissed from service. She believed her husband was tricked into enlisting in the Marine Corps and she was left with two small children whom she could not support. Mrs. Stinger stated her case in a letter dated August 31, 1812, complaining that her husband was drunk when he enlisted.

. . . Daniel Stinger, a Baker by trade, enlisted in the City of Philadelphia, as a Marine in the service of the

The USS *Constitution*, the pride of the U.S. Navy's fleet during the War of 1812. This image and others can be found at the **USS *Constitution*** Web site of the Naval Historical Center.

United States. that at the time he enlisted he was so much under the influence of liquor as to be incapable of knowing what he did. that the enlisting officer took advantage of his intoxication when he persuaded him to enlist and that he had not recovered from the effects of the liquor when he took the Oath. . . .

Jane Stinger then offered to ". . . willingly sacrifice a part of her furniture with which to procure the means of providing a substitute in the place of her husband."[6]

Letters and Diaries From British Subjects

One of the most captivating stories of the war involves Laura Secord, who risked her life and became a true Canadian heroine. American soldiers took over her home, and one night she overheard them boast about secret plans to launch a surprise attack on British headquarters twenty miles away. Secord had to make a grueling walk to alert Lieutenant James FitzGibbon at the British outpost at Beaver Dams. Her warning helped FitzGibbon defeat an entire American regiment.

Almost fifty years later, Secord finally gave her account of that journey:

I found I should have great difficulty in getting through the American guards. . . . Determined to persevere, however, I left early in the morning, walked nineteen miles in the month of June, over a rough and difficult part of the country . . . Here I found all the Indians encamped; by moonlight the scene was terrifying. . . .

The chief at first objected to let me pass, but finally consented, after some hesitation, to go with me and accompany me to Fitzgibbon's station which was at the Beaver Dam, where I had an interview with him. I then told him what I had come for, and what I had heard. . . . Capt. Fitzgibbon formed his plan accordingly, and captured about five hundred American infantry, about fifty mounted dragoons. . . . I returned home next day, exhausted and fatigued. [7]

Robert Dickson was a Canadian fur trader who later became an Indian agent. His nickname was the Red-Haired Man, and he helped Britain recruit Indian tribes to fight against Americans. In a letter

The War of 1812: People - Microsoft Internet Explorer

File   Edit   View   Favorites   Tools   Help

Address http://www.galafilm.com/1812/e/catalogues/peop_secord.html

Laura Secord, Canadian

The combatants in a war are not the only ones involved. Canadian Laura Secord, a civilian, risked her life to warn the British of an impending American attack. Her story and those of others can be found on the **Galafilm War of 1812** Web site.

to the commander in chief of British forces, dated December 23, 1812, Dickson listed items that were needed to secure the cooperation of the various Indian tribes, including

> A large Wampum Belt with proper designations & an appropriate speech, encouraging a general and spirited combination, among the different Indian Tribes . . . Canoes . . . Twenty young men as Interpreters . . . One silk Standard & one large medal to be got for each Tribe.[8]

Amelia Harris was a Canadian woman who recalled a raid at dawn on her mother's farm by American soldiers in May 1814. She wrote of the despair they felt.

> . . . as my Mother and myself were at breakfast, the Dogs made an unusual barking. I went to the door to discover the cause. When I looked up I saw the hillside and the fields as the eye could reach covered with American soldiers. They had landed at Patterson's Creek. Burnt the Mills and village of Port Dover. . . .
>
> Two men . . . came into the room where we were standing and took coals from the hearth, without speaking. My mother knew instinctively what they were going to do. She . . . asked to see the commanding officer. . . . She entreated him to spare her property and said that she was a widow with a young family. He answered her civilly & respectfully and regretted that his orders were to Burn, but that He would spare the house, which he did. . . .

Very soon we saw a column of dark smoke arise from every Building and what at early morn had been a prosperous homestead, at noon there remained only smouldering ruins. . . It would not be easy to describe my mother's feelings as she looked at the desolation around her.[9]

Patrick Finan was twelve years old when he left for Kingston, on Lake Ontario, by steamboat with his family. In his journal, he recorded an ambush by American soldiers:

As the balls were flying about us, perforating the sides of the boats . . . great confusion prevailed . . . our only alternative was to leap into the water, and make . . . our way to it [the shore]. I had a full view of . . . women screaming, children bawling, officers commanding, but all endeavoring to get out of reach of the shot as fast as possible.[10]

The following is part of a personal account by the wife of a junior officer in the British Army serving in Kingston in 1814. Although she did not name herself, the woman wrote about how the war affected her life and her child. She described how she had tried to slip onto a ship, the *Woodpecker,* to accompany her husband on a mission, but the captain ordered her off and the vessel sailed away.

I would not let myself possibly think how long it would be before we were to meet again but I did not and would not despair. . . . Standing under the growing clouds of a stormy evening on a wharf crowded with soldiers and Sailors with baggage and myself the only female in sight and my poor child sleeping in my arms and the only human being upon whom I had depended now flying from us . . . I stood still for a moment watching the receding sail of the *Woodpecker,* trying to collect my thoughts and decide what next was to be done.[11]

Her thoughts undoubtedly echoed those of many other military families, on both sides, who struggled during the war.

THE WAR IN SONG AND POETRY

Songs and poems reflected the mood of the time as well as the need to raise morale in battle. The war's music ranged from rousing military field marches performed with fifes and drums to the hundreds of songs that were written to inspire patriotism.

▶ More Than Just Tunes

Fifers and drummers provided an important source of communication during the war, not only on the battlefield but also in camp. Their music signaled times for the soldiers' daily routines: when to wake up, when to eat, and even when to sleep. These musicians also provided a rhythm for marching. During the smoky haze of battle, the sounding of the drum told troops when to advance, when to retreat, and when to fire their guns. It was during this war that a military bugle was first used. Its strong,

Star-Spangled Banner and the War of 1812

Access this Web site from http://www.myreportlinks.com

This Smithsonian Institution site offers images of the flag that flew over Fort McHenry during the War of 1812 and inspired Francis Scott Key to write "The Star-Spangled Banner."

clear sound signaled commands that were heard throughout the camp and over the noise of battle.[1]

"O Say Can You See"

Most Americans today are not familiar with the songs that were written during the War of 1812. However, the war did inspire one famous song that Americans still sing. It is the national anthem, "The Star-Spangled Banner." But it began as a poem, "Defence of Fort McHenry," written by Francis Scott Key in September 1814 about the huge American flag that flew above Fort McHenry, Maryland. First published with four verses, it did not become the official anthem of the United States until March 3, 1931.

Francis Scott Key, a thirty-five-year-old attorney, had the misfortune to be aboard an enemy ship in Chesapeake Bay. One of Key's friends had been taken prisoner by the British, and Key and an American government agent had gone to the ship to arrange a prisoner exchange. Since the Royal Navy was about to bombard Fort McHenry, Key and the others were not allowed to leave until after the battle. Key witnessed the British attack throughout the stormy night of September 13, 1814. He kept his eye on the giant American flag that waved above the fort. The flag had been made ". . . so large that the British will have no difficulty in seeing it from a distance," according to the fort's commander, Major George Armistead.[2] It measured thirty feet by forty-two feet, nearly three stories tall. Mary Pickersgill, a

▲ *This print depicts Key with right arm outstretched toward the flag flying over Fort McHenry.*

widow who made extra money by making flags for Baltimore's ships, sewed the flag bearing fifteen stripes and fifteen stars that flew from the fort.

Key scribbled a poem on the back of a letter he had in his pocket that described his impressions and emotions of that night. He had the poem printed and distributed, and it soon became popular. It was set to the tune of an old English drinking song, "Anacreon in Heaven." The first stanza of "The Star-Spangled Banner" is sung as our national anthem.

O say can you see, by the dawn's early light,
What so proudly we hail'd at the twilight's last gleaming.
Whose broad stripes and bright stars through the perilous fight
O'er the ramparts we watch'd were so gallantly streaming?
And the rocket's red glare, the bombs bursting in air,
Gave proof through the night that our flag was still there,
O say does that star-spangled banner yet wave
O'er the land of the free and the home of the brave?[3]

▶ Songs for the Navy

A variety of patriotic songs were written, published, and performed by both sides during the war. They were intended to encourage a feeling of national pride and unity and to boost support for this unpopular war. Songs were published in newspapers, broadsides (large posters containing advertisements), or in songbooks.

Many popular songs documented the first five naval battles that the United States won, beginning with the famous duel of August 19, 1812, between the *Constitution*, under Captain Isaac Hull, and the *Guerrière*, under Captain James Dacres. There were countless songs with

I Hear America Singing: "Star-Spangled Banner"

Access this Web site from http://www.myreportlinks.com

This Library of Congress site contains images of various versions of the poem composed during the War of 1812 that became our national anthem.

the same title, "The *Constitution* and The *Guerrière*."
One lively version describes the surrender of Captain
James Dacres.

> *Then Dacres came on board,*
> *To deliver up his sword,*
> *Tho' loath he was to part with it,'twas handy, oh!*
> *"Oh, keep your sword," says Hull,*
> *"For it only makes you dull,*
> *Cheer up and let us have a little brandy, oh!"*[4]

A painting of Captain Isaac Hull, the commander of the USS *Constitution*, from **The Mariners' Museum: The Naval War of 1812.**

Another tribute, "Ye Parliament of England," was an add-on song: Verses were added to it with each naval victory. It ends with this warning:

Lament you sons of Britain, for distant is the day,
When you'll regain by British force what you lost in Americay.
Go tell your King and Parliament by all the world 'tis known
The British force by sea and land by Yankees is o'er thrown.[5]

A witty song poked fun at the British who failed to blockade the coast of Stonington, Connecticut. Here are a few stanzas from "The Battle of Stonington":

Their bombs were thrown, their rockets flew,
And not a man of all their crew
Though every man stood full in view,
Could kill a man of Stonington.

They killed a goose, they killed a hen,
Three hogs they wounded in a pen;
They dashed away—and pray, what then?
That was not taking Stonington.[6]

▷ Songs for the Army

There were songs for every major battle including "The Heroes of Queenstown," "The Battle of Lundy's Lane," and "The Battle of Baltimore." General Andrew Jackson became a larger-than-life national hero after he defeated the British at New Orleans. Samuel Woodworth, a famous songwriter, wrote

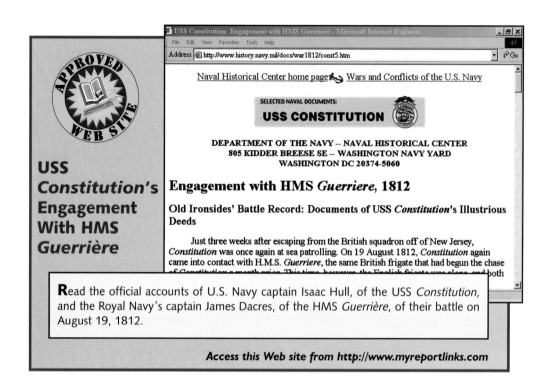

USS
Constitution's
Engagement
With HMS
Guerrière

USS CONSTITUTION

DEPARTMENT OF THE NAVY -- NAVAL HISTORICAL CENTER
805 KIDDER BREESE SE -- WASHINGTON NAVY YARD
WASHINGTON DC 20374-5060

Engagement with HMS *Guerriere*, 1812

Old Ironsides' Battle Record: Documents of USS *Constitution*'s Illustrious Deeds

Just three weeks after escaping from the British squadron off of New Jersey, *Constitution* was once again at sea patrolling. On 19 August 1812, *Constitution* again came into contact with H.M.S. *Guerriere*, the same British frigate that had begun the chase

Read the official accounts of U.S. Navy captain Isaac Hull, of the USS *Constitution*, and the Royal Navy's captain James Dacres, of the HMS *Guerrière*, of their battle on August 19, 1812.

Access this Web site from http://www.myreportlinks.com

"The Hunters of Kentucky" to honor Jackson and his frontier sharpshooters. One stanza brags

We are a hardy, free-born race; each man to fear a stranger;
Whate'er the game we join in chase, despising time and danger;
And if a daring foe annoys, whate'er his strength and forces,
We'll show him that Kentucky boys are alligator horses.[7]

Other songs spoke of yearnings that went beyond the battle. During the war, some African-American slaves met in secret. At their meetings, they voiced their hope that a British victory would help them become free men since the slave trade had been abolished in Great Britain in 1807. At those meetings, they sometimes sang this eloquent hymn, "Hail! Africa Band," in anticipation of freedom.

> Hail! All hail! Ye Afric clan!
> Hail! Ye oppressed, ye Afric band!
> Who toil and sweat in slavery bound,
> Who toil and sweat in slavery bound,
> And when your health and strength are gone
> Are left to hunger and to mourn.
> Let Independence be your aim,
> Ever mindful what 'tis worth;
> Pledge your bodies for the prize,
> Pile them even to the skies![8]

▶ British and Canadian Songs and Poems

One of Upper Canada's patriotic songs, "The Noble Lads of Canada," rallied the troops:

> Oh, now the time has come, my boys, to cross the Yankee line,
> We remember they were rebels once, and conquered John
>   Burgoyne;
> We'll subdue those mighty Democrats, and pull their dwellings
>   down,
> And we'll have the States inhabited with subjects to the
>   crown.[9]

General John Burgoyne was the British commander who surrendered to American forces at Saratoga during the Revolutionary War.

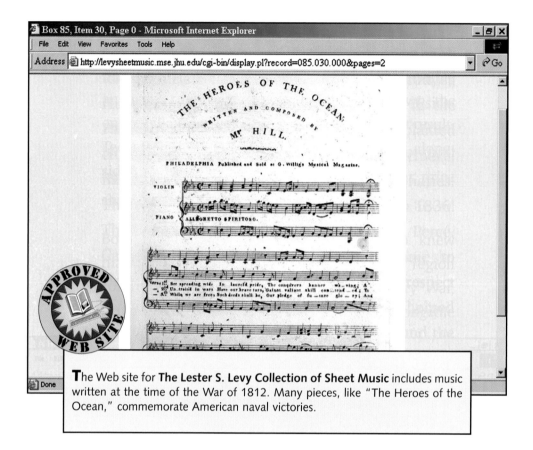

The Web site for **The Lester S. Levy Collection of Sheet Music** includes music written at the time of the War of 1812. Many pieces, like "The Heroes of the Ocean," commemorate American naval victories.

"The Maple Leaf Forever," a song well known to Canadian schoolchildren, was written more than half a century after the War of 1812. Referring to one of Canada's national symbols, it became an unofficial national anthem.

At Queenston Heights and Lundy's Lane,
Our brave fathers, side by side,
For freedom, homes and loved ones dear,
Firmly stood and nobly died;
And those dear rights which they maintained,
We swear to yield them never!

Our watchword ever more shall be,
The Maple Leaf forever![10]

General William Hull surrendered Detroit to Major General Sir Isaac Brock. "The Bold Canadians" celebrates Brock's triumph.

Come all ye bold Canadians,
I'd have you lend an ear,
Unto a short ditty
Which will your spirits cheer,
Concerning an engagement
We had at Detroit town,
The pride of those Yankee boys
So bravely we pulled down.[11]

"The *Shannon* and The *Chesapeake*" commemorates a British naval victory. The British commander of the *Shannon*, Captain Sir Philip Bowes Vere Broke, challenged the *Chesapeake* under Captain James Lawrence "ship to ship."

Now the Chesapeake *so bold sailed from Boston we've*
been told,
For to take the British frigate neat and handy, O!
The people in the port all came out to see the sport
And the bands were playing "Yankee Doodle Dandy," O!

Here's a health, brave Broke, to you, to your officers
and crew,
Who aboard the Shannon *frigate fought so handy-o;*

Niagara to Stoney Creek

Access this Web site from http://www.myreportlinks.com

Although Queenston Heights was a British victory, it was won at great cost: Major General Isaac Brock was killed early in the fighting. Niagara to Stoney Creek, a Canadian museum Web site, offers details of the battle.

And may it always prove, that in fighting and in love, The British tar forever is the dandy-o.[12]

Tar is another name for a sailor.

"A Ballad for Brave Women" is a stirring tribute to Laura Secord, a Canadian heroine of the War of 1812. This poem later set to music tells of her risky twenty-mile journey to warn the British of a surprise attack by American forces.

> *A story worth telling, our annals afford,*
> *'This the wonderful journey of Laura Secord!*
> *Her poor crippled spouse hobbled home*
> > *With the news*
> *That Boerstler was nigh: "Not a minute to lose,*
> *Not an instant," said Laura, "for stoppage or pause–*
> *I must hurry and warn our brave troops at Decaws."*[13]

Colonel Boerstler was the commander of American forces in Queenston.

PRESS COVERAGE
OF THE WAR

In 1809 there were about 329 newspapers in the United States. By the end of the war, in 1815, the number had grown to 413.[1] The press of the time was not objective or neutral when reporting the war or other political issues. Newspapers were openly biased and published the views of the political party that their editors supported.

The *National Intelligencer,* published in Washington, was the unofficial voice of the Madison administration and favored going to war. Joseph Gales, Jr., was the publisher of this major daily paper, which recorded the opinions of President Madison and his cabinet. Northern newspapers and many papers from the middle and southern states were mostly Federalist and published editorials opposing war. The *New York Evening Post* was one of the leading Federalist papers. A political paper, *Niles' Weekly Register,* came out in 1811 as a competitor. Published in Baltimore, Maryland, by Hezekiah Niles, the paper claimed to be neutral, giving balanced views of the issues of the day.

▶ Baltimore Riots

The heated stories in partisan newspapers sparked a riot in Baltimore in the summer of 1812. Just two days after war was declared, the *Federal Republican* condemned the war. In a defiant editorial published on June 20, 1812, the newspaper declared,

> Without funds, without taxes, without an army, navy, or adequate fortifications . . . our rulers have promulged [decreed] a war against the clear and decided sentiments of a vast majority of the nation. . . . We mean to represent in as strong colors as we are capable, that it [the war] is unnecessary, inexpedient [not advisable] . . . We are avowedly hostile to the presidency of James Madison.[2]

An angry mob that supported the war attacked the news office. The defenders of the paper nearly

▲ Political cartoons about the war were often comical and vicious at the same time. In "Columbia teaching John Bull his new lesson," America's relationship with both Great Britain and France is satirized. America is represented by Columbia, Great Britain by John Bull, and France by "Mounseer Beau Napperty" (Napoléon Bonaparte, the emperor of France).

beat several people to death and shot some of the attackers. The news staff was sent to jail for protection, and the crowd then stormed the jail. The militia eventually restored order.

On Going to War

Long before Congress declared war on June 18, 1812, the nation was divided on whether or not to go to war. The *National Intelligencer* favored going to war to preserve national honor. On April 14, 1812, it ran an editorial titled "War Should Be Declared," which stated:

> ...where is the motive for longer delay? The final step ought to be taken, and that step is WAR. ... Our wrongs have been great; our cause is just; and if we are decided and firm, success is inevitable. ... Let war therefore be forthwith proclaimed against England.[3]

The *New York Evening Post* opposed going to war to annex Canada, stating that it was a waste of manpower and money. On April 21, 1812, the *Post* declared,

> Citizens ... the measure is perfect madness. You will lose millions when you will gain a cent. The expense will be enormous. It will ruin our country. ... Will you spend thousands of millions in conquering a province which, were it made a present to us, would not be worth accepting? Our territories are already too large.[4]

On the issue of impressment of American seamen by the Royal Navy, the *Centinel of Freedom,* published in Newark, New Jersey, had this to say on June 2, 1812:

> How degrading these things appear . . . If we profess to be Americans, we must shield those *Liberties* which are our natural rights . . . man-stealing is in future to be considered by our government as *piracy* and *felony*—and the perpetrators upon conviction, to suffer death.[5]

The sentiments of New England Federalists about war were summed up by the *Connecticut*

△ *William Charles is considered America's first political cartoonist for his caricatures of figures involved in the War of 1812. Here, King George III is bested by James Madison in "A boxing match, or another bloody nose for John Bull," the cartoonist's take on the defeat of the British warship* Boxer *by the American frigate* Enterprise.

Courant on June 30, 1812: It "was commenced in folly, it is proposed to be carried on with madness, and (unless speedily terminated) will end in ruin."[6]

News of the Battles

Newspapers kept readers informed about battles and other related events. Press reports about land battles were not encouraging because the United States Army and American militia suffered many defeats. Newspapers continued their political bias. The Republican papers emphasized the victories and downplayed the defeats, and the Federalist papers emphasized the defeats and continued to criticize the war. When covering naval battles, the press published countless stories praising American victories on the lakes and the seas.

Newspapers of the time freely published information on military operations that included troop locations and offensive and defensive plans. This practice would have been even more damaging to the American fighting forces if communications had not been so slow. There was one unusual episode in which an American newspaper tipped off the British by publishing details of the United States Navy's plans. The *National Intelligencer* published a letter dated May 20, 1813, concerning the construction of warships for Commodore Oliver Perry. It described the three gunboats already armed and on the water and said that two more were waiting to be launched. The paper reported that the canvas for the ships' sails

. . . will be in Pittsburgh by the 25th of this month, therefore we cannot rely on it before the middle of June. General [William Henry] Harrison is not expected to move [north] before we get command of the lake. We are apprehensive, what with one delay after another, it will be fall before he can move against Detroit.[7]

The British did not need spies when American newspapers gave such complete details.[8]

One common thread that united most newspapers was their hatred of Great Britain. Newspapers

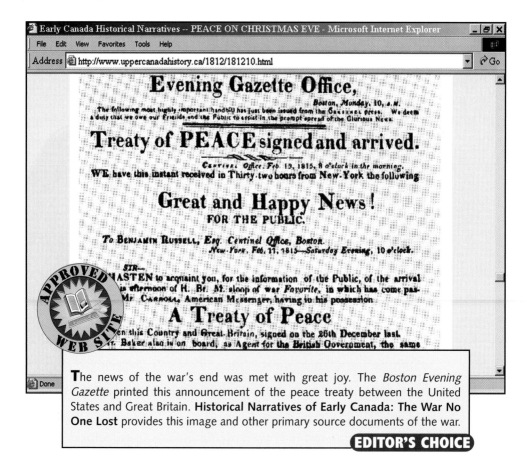

Early Canada Historical Narratives -- PEACE ON CHRISTMAS EVE - Microsoft Internet Explorer

File   Edit   View   Favorites   Tools   Help

Address http://www.uppercanadahistory.ca/1812/181210.html

Evening Gazette Office,

Boston, Monday, 10, A.M.

The following most highly important handbill has just been issued from the Centinel press. We deem it a duty that we owe our Friends and the Public to assist in the prompt spread of the Glorious News.

Treaty of PEACE signed and arrived.

Centinel Office, Feb. 13, 1815, 8 o'clock in the morning.

WE have this instant received in Thirty-two hours from New-York the following

Great and Happy News!
FOR THE PUBLIC.

To BENJAMIN RUSSELL, Esq. Centinel Office, Boston.

New-York, Feb. 11, 1815—Saturday Evening, 10 o'clock.

SIR—

HASTEN to acquaint you, for the information of the Public, of the arrival this afternoon of H. Br. M. sloop of war Favorite, in which has come passenger Mr. CARROLL, American Messenger, having in his possession

A Treaty of Peace

between this Country and Great Britain, signed on the 20th December last. Mr. Baker also is on board, as Agent for the British Government, the same

Done

The news of the war's end was met with great joy. The *Boston Evening Gazette* printed this announcement of the peace treaty between the United States and Great Britain. **Historical Narratives of Early Canada: The War No One Lost** provides this image and other primary source documents of the war.

EDITOR'S CHOICE

often printed vicious editorials about the British government. Hezekiah Niles, on October 30, 1813, blasted England as

the common robber, the man-stealer, the scalper of women and children and prisoners . . . the enemy of our fathers . . . the cause of every war that has afflicted the civilized world for fifty years past, the common pest of society and plague of the earth . . . the cold-calculating assassin of thirty million people in *India,* the ferocious murderer in Ireland, the minister of famine and pestilence [sic] in America . . . a government so polluted . . . that it must perish of its own action, sooner or later . . . [A] nation red to her arm-pits in the blood of innocents.[9]

▷ Peace at Last

When the Treaty of Ghent was signed, members of both parties claimed victory. The Federalists felt that the original aims of the war had not been achieved through the peace treaty and therefore their antiwar beliefs had been proven. Republicans looked at the peace treaty as a triumph for America and felt vindicated. Americans were still divided over the results of the war.

The *New York Evening Post* summed up the results with this verse:

Your commerce is wantonly lost,
Your treasures are wasted and gone;
You've fought to no end, but with millions of cost,

And for rivers of blood you've nothing to boast
But credit and nation undone.[10]

The New York *National Advocate* echoed the Republicans in this article printed on February 17, 1815, which began "Cold and unfeeling must be that man who thinks we have gained nothing by the present war. If there exists such an animal in the bosom of our country, suspect him." The editorial continued:

The republic is safe. . . . we have beaten and discomfited that enemy by sea and by land; and . . . have humbled him in dust and ashes, and thus strengthened and consolidated our empire. This object, therefore, has been accomplished by the war.[11]

▷ From the Canadian Press

Canadian papers carried news of the war that included the personal stories of people involved. One account published in the Quebec *Gazette* on July 15, 1813, reported how two Canadian women had helped a British officer. Mrs. Kirby and Mrs. Dunfield lived near Fort George, on the Niagara peninsula, an area of Canada occupied by American forces. When Lieutenant James FitzGibbon was attacked by a group of American soldiers, they came to his aid, according to this newspaper account.

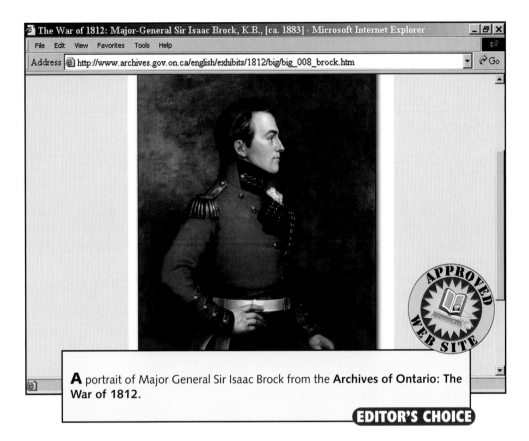

A portrait of Major General Sir Isaac Brock from the **Archives of Ontario: The War of 1812.**

EDITOR'S CHOICE

Lieut[enant] Fitzgibbon called upon two men who were looking on, to assist him in disarming the two Americans, but they would not interfere; poor Mrs. Kirby apparently distracted, used all her influence, but in vain; the rifleman finding that he could not disengage his piece, drew F's sword . . . when another woman, a Mrs. Dunfield seized the uplifted arm and wrested the sword from his grasp . . . a young boy, 13 years old, . . . was very useful in the struggle which continued for some minutes.[12]

Major General Isaac Brock was the commander of the land and naval forces in Canada, and his military skill and bold leadership inspired his men. Born in England, Brock is considered the first Canadian hero. When he was killed at the Battle of Queenston Heights, the Quebec *Gazette* was but one of many newspapers that praised him.

> The news of the death of this excellent officer has been received here as a public calamity. . . . His long residence in this province . . . had made him in habits and good offices almost a citizen; and his frankness, conciliatory disposition, and elevated demeanour, an estimable one. The expressions of regret . . . not only by grown persons, but young children, are the test of his worth.[13]

▶ From the British Press

At the war's beginning, British newspapers criticized going to war against the United States. That changed once Britain ended its war against France and focused its energies on the United States. The *Times* of London on October 29, 1812, gave this advice on how to conduct the war:

> The paramount duty . . . is to render the English arms as formidable in the new world as they have become in the old. . . . Our plans of hostility . . . ought not to be confined to the North [Canada]. On the contrary, we should contrive as much as is consistent with our own safety, to spare the inhabitants of New York and New England, who are reluctantly dragged into the war. The southern states, on the contrary, as they have

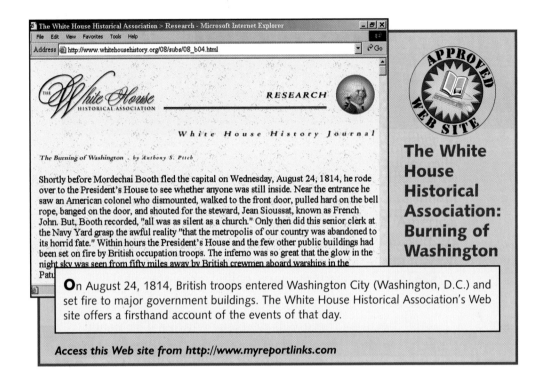

The White House Historical Association > Research - Microsoft Internet Explorer

File   Edit   View   Favorites   Tools   Help

Address http://www.whitehousehistory.org/08/subs/08_b04.html   Go

THE White House
HISTORICAL ASSOCIATION

RESEARCH

White House History Journal

The Burning of Washington , *by Anthony S. Pitch*

Shortly before Mordechai Booth fled the capital on Wednesday, August 24, 1814, he rode over to the President's House to see whether anyone was still inside. Near the entrance he saw an American colonel who dismounted, walked to the front door, pulled hard on the bell rope, banged on the door, and shouted for the steward, Jean Sioussat, known as French John. But, Booth recorded, "all was as silent as a church." Only then did this senior clerk at the Navy Yard grasp the awful reality "that the metropolis of our country was abandoned to its horrid fate." Within hours the President's House and the few other public buildings had been set on fire by British occupation troops. The inferno was so great that the glow in the night sky was seen from fifty miles away by British crewmen aboard warships in the Patu

APPROVED WEB SITE

The White House Historical Association: Burning of Washington

On August 24, 1814, British troops entered Washington City (Washington, D.C.) and set fire to major government buildings. The White House Historical Association's Web site offers a firsthand account of the events of that day.

Access this Web site from http://www.myreportlinks.com

most cordially embraced the mischievous politics of the President, ought to receive their richly merited reward. [14]

The British often read American newspapers to learn about the war. Rear Admiral George Cockburn had developed a personal hatred toward Joseph Gales because he thought the editor published distorted accounts in the *National Intelligencer* about the admiral's raids. When the British invaded Washington, Cockburn personally supervised the destruction of the newspaper office and presses. He gave this order: "Be sure that all the C's in the boxes are destroyed, so that the rascals can have no further means of abusing my name."[15]

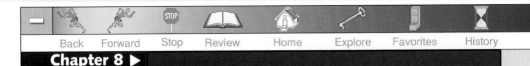
DID ANYONE REALLY WIN?

God looks after little children, idiots, drunken sailors, and the United States of America.

—Old proverb[1]

Some historians have called the War of 1812 "the war nobody won" and "the war that both sides won" because there was no clear winner. The peace treaty consisted of eleven articles and three thousand words, but it did not solve the conflicts that had led to war. There was no mention of territorial gains on either side nor was there any mention of shipping rights, the impressment problem, or American Indian issues. Each party to the war was convinced that it had won.

▶ Peace for the United States

For the United States, news of peace was greeted with parades and celebrations. The nation was tired of war. The cost was high. Official figures from the Department of Defense show that 286,730 military personnel served, with 2,260 killed and 4,505 wounded.[2] One historian, Donald R. Hickey, claims that even those official sources are not reliable and that 528,000 American troops served, including

57,000 regulars, 10,000 volunteers, 3,000 rangers, and 458,000 militia. Another 20,000 served in the U.S. Navy and Marines. Furthermore, he suggests the casualty figures do not

The Cabildo: The Battle of New Orleans

Access this Web site from http://www.myreportlinks.com

This Louisiana State Museum Web site provides information on the last major battle of the War of 1812 and contains images of historical documents, maps, and artifacts from the museum's collection.

EDITOR'S CHOICE

include deaths from disease, which could have been two and one half times the total of battle deaths. Hickey estimates that the war cost the United States $158,000,000.[3]

Still, how the war ended accomplished a great deal. For the United States, there was a new sense of national pride. The war changed how Americans viewed their country. The United States was no longer a loose union of separate states. This feeling of national unity was described in a letter that Albert Gallatin, secretary of the treasury and peace negotiator, wrote to Thomas Jefferson in 1815:

> The war has renewed and reinstated the national feelings and character which the Revolution had given, and which were daily lessened. The people now have more general objects of attachment with which their pride and political opinions are connected. They are more Americans; they feel and act more as a nation.[4]

Andrew Jackson: War of 1812 and the Battle of New Orleans

Access this Web site from http://www.myreportlinks.com

On America's Story from America's Library, a Library of Congress Web site, you will find articles about General Andrew Jackson and the Battle of New Orleans, fought after a peace treaty was signed.

The war also had other results. Americans learned that they could not depend on local militias for national defense. Instead, America planned to build a first-rate army led by trained professional officers. However, it was not until World War I that a large professional army was established. Congress also voted to build twenty-one new warships to strengthen the navy.

Americans continued to push farther west to settle in the Ohio and the Mississippi River valleys, areas occupied by American Indians. White settlers wanted this land because it was fertile. They cleared trees, built cabins, and planted crops, causing misery to the native people who wanted to remain in their homelands.

New technology and the growth of industry began to change the way Americans lived. Factories were built and new machines for cotton mills developed. New England became an industrial center.

In national politics, the Federalist party, which had opposed the war, began its decline. The United States entered a period known as the "era of good feelings" because there were few political arguments within political parties. A military historian, John Elting, sums up the outcome of the war this way:

> In cold fact the United States survived only because handfuls of American soldiers and sailors, ill-supported and finally almost abandoned by their central government, ignored and often betrayed by their fellow countrymen, somehow made head against all odds until England at last wearied.[5]

▶ Peace for Great Britain

When it became clear that it could not win, the British government became anxious for peace. But London newspapers blasted the terms of the treaty and England's handling of the war. The *Times* of London called the treaty "deadly" and "disgraceful." The *Morning Chronicle* criticized British leaders who had ". . . humbled themselves in the dust" and "thereby brought discredit on the country."[6]

The War of 1812 was not as significant an event in Great Britain as its victory over Napoléon and France was. As historian Fred L. Engelman notes, "To the British it was a relatively minor affair . . . Except for the hatred which the war had increased and for the necessity of attending to the problems which the treaty had not solved, the British soon virtually forgot the whole affair."[7]

Peace for Canada

For Canadians, the war had been a matter of national survival. Canadians believed they won because they and the British kept the United States out of their country. A Canadian historian, William Wood, writes, "The one really decisive and lasting naval and military result of the war was the complete British victory over the third unsuccessful American invasion of Canada."[8]

The war divided the North American continent and helped create a new Canadian national identity. Historian Donald R. Hickey explains.

In 1812 the various provinces in Canada were little more than outposts in the British Empire populated by a jarring combination of French Canadians, native-born British subjects, Loyalists who had fled from the United States during the Revolution, and Americans who had migrated across the border in search of greater economic opportunities. The War of 1812 helped cement these disparate groups into a nation.[9]

This new sense of nationalism made Canadians suspicious of American ideas. According to Canadian historian Pierre Berton, Canadians decided to adopt the British, not American, way of life. He credits that idea to John Strachan, a Loyalist who was the bishop of York. Berton calls Strachan a true "Canadian hero." Strachan went on to become an important political leader. Of Strachan,

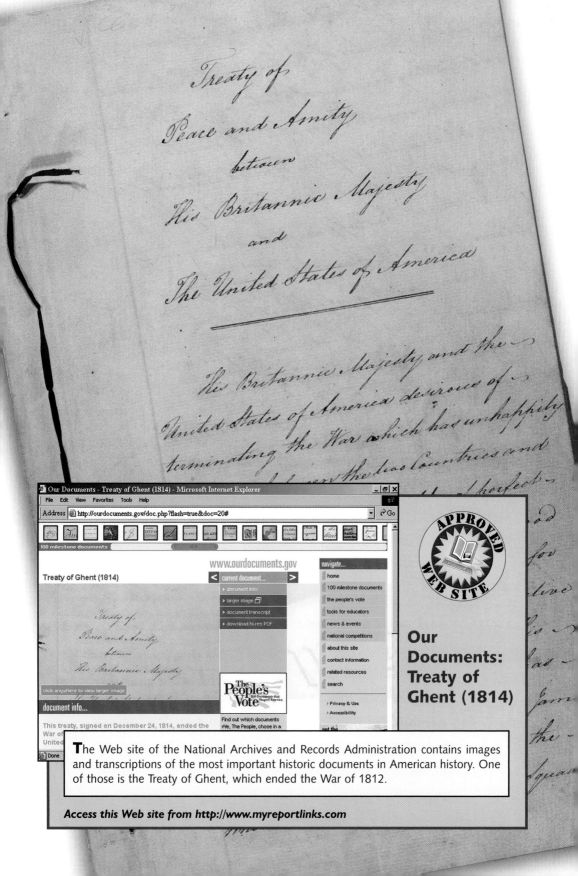

Treaty of

Peace and Amity

between

His Britannic Majesty

and

The United States of America

The Web site of the National Archives and Records Administration contains images and transcriptions of the most important historic documents in American history. One of those is the Treaty of Ghent, which ended the War of 1812.

Access this Web site from http://www.myreportlinks.com

Berton says, "He despised Americans, loathed Americanisms. 'Democracy' and 'republicanism' were hateful words." Instead, Strachan wanted Upper Canada to be purely British. Berton concludes, "Few Canadians found it possible to consider, at least openly, the American way as a political choice for the future."[10]

Another Canadian historian, C. P. Stacey, has this to say about the end of the war:

> The War of 1812 is one of those episodes in history that make everybody happy, because everybody interprets it in his own way. The Americans think of it primarily as a naval war in which the pride of the Mistress of the Seas was humbled. . . . Canadians think of it equally pridefully as a war of defence in which their brave fathers . . . saved the country from conquest. And the English are the happiest of all because they don't even know it existed.[11]

▶ "Peace" for American Indians

The American Indians were the ones who lost the most with the outcome of the war. Although they had fought in its battles, they were not invited to participate in the peace talks.

American Indians fought for tribal survival and freedom to roam the plains and forests. War was a last attempt to reclaim their lost land. The attempt failed and so did the idea of an American Indian confederacy. After the war, the native warriors and

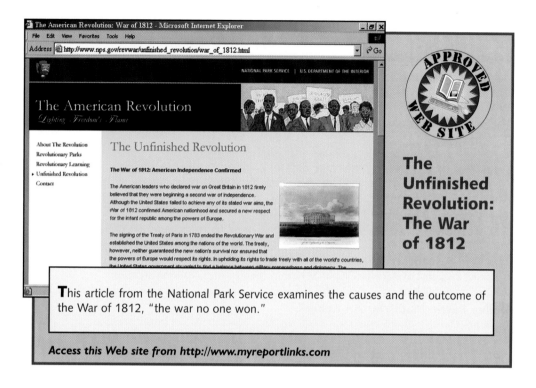

The American Revolution: War of 1812 - Microsoft Internet Explorer

File Edit View Favorites Tools Help

Address http://www.nps.gov/revwar/unfinished_revolution/war_of_1812.html   Go

NATIONAL PARK SERVICE | U.S. DEPARTMENT OF THE INTERIOR

The American Revolution
Lighting Freedom's Flame

About The Revolution
Revolutionary Parks
Revolutionary Learning
▸ Unfinished Revolution
Contact

The Unfinished Revolution

The War of 1812: American Independence Confirmed

The American leaders who declared war on Great Britain in 1812 firmly believed that they were beginning a second war of independence. Although the United States failed to achieve any of its stated war aims, the War of 1812 confirmed American nationhood and secured a new respect for the infant republic among the powers of Europe.

The signing of the Treaty of Paris in 1783 ended the Revolutionary War and established the United States among the nations of the world. The treaty, however, neither guaranteed the new nation's survival nor ensured that the powers of Europe would respect its rights. In upholding its rights to trade freely with all of the world's countries, the United States government struggled to find a balance between military preparedness and diplomacy. The

The Unfinished Revolution: The War of 1812

This article from the National Park Service examines the causes and the outcome of the War of 1812, "the war no one won."

Access this Web site from http://www.myreportlinks.com

their families lost their lands and much of the freedom they once had.

When Black Hawk, the Sauk and Fox chief, heard the details of the peace treaty, it was reported that he wept. He declared, "I have fought the Big Knives [American frontiersmen] and will continue to fight them, until they retire from our lands."[12] In 1832, the Black Hawk War continued Tecumseh's dream of creating a confederacy of American Indian nations. But that, too, was doomed when the American government's policy of Indian removal forced America's native people west.

Report Links

The Internet sites described below can be accessed at http://www.myreportlinks.com

Archives of Ontario: The War of 1812
Editor's Choice View this Canadian collection of documents, maps, and images of the war.

Historical Narratives of Early Canada: The War No One Lost
Editor's Choice A Canadian educator presents narratives from the War of 1812.

Treasures of Congress: The War of 1812—The Capitol in Flames
Editor's Choice Find documents about the burning of Washington, D.C., at this site.

The Cabildo: The Battle of New Orleans
Editor's Choice Learn about the Battle of New Orleans from this Louisiana Web site.

The James Madison Center: War of 1812
Editor's Choice Explore the War of 1812 through the James Madison archives.

Dolley Payne Madison: An Exhibit
Editor's Choice At this university site, learn more about the life of Dolley Madison.

American Military History: The War of 1812
Read an excerpt about the War of 1812 from a military history book.

The American President: James Madison
Read a biography of President James Madison.

The American War of 1812
This university site contains journal entries and newspaper articles dealing with the war.

Andrew Jackson: War of 1812 and the Battle of New Orleans
This Library of Congress site offers information on Andrew Jackson and the Battle of New Orleans.

The Avalon Project at Yale Law School: The War of 1812
Yale University's Avalon Project offers primary source documents from the War of 1812.

▶**Canada Before the War of 1812**
This site examines Canadian history before and during the war.

Galafilm War of 1812
Biographies, images, documents, and more of the war are presented by this site.

I Hear America Singing: "Star-Spangled Banner"
View various editions of "The Star-Spangled Banner."

The James Madison Center—Tecumseh: An American Hero
Read about the life of the Shawnee chief Tecumseh, who sided with the British during the war.

Report Links

The Internet sites described below can be accessed at
http://www.myreportlinks.com

The Lester S. Levy Collection of Sheet Music
Explore this collection of popular American sheet music from the War of 1812 era.

The Mariners' Museum: The Naval War of 1812
This museum site provides a historic look at the U.S. Navy in the War of 1812.

Named Campaigns—The War of 1812
The U.S. Army Center of Military History Web site offers an overview of the battles of the war.

Naval Historical Center: Officers in the War of 1812
View a list of men who served during the War of 1812.

Niagara to Stoney Creek
Learn about the Battle of Stoney Creek on this Web site from the Battlefield House Museum.

Ohio History Central: War of 1812
Read a brief overview of the War of 1812 on this Web site.

Our Atlases: The War of 1812
Battle maps of the war can be viewed at this West Point site.

Our Documents: Treaty of Ghent (1814)
View an archival copy of the Treaty of Ghent, which ended the War of 1812.

Star-Spangled Banner and the War of 1812
Learn about the flag that inspired our national anthem.

The Unfinished Revolution: The War of 1812
Read an article about the War of 1812.

U.S. Brig *Niagara:* Oliver Hazard Perry
Read about Oliver Hazard Perry and the Battle of Lake Erie.

USS *Constitution*
Learn about the history of "Old Ironsides" and its role in the War of 1812.

USS *Constitution*'s Engagement With HMS *Guerrière.*
Learn about the 1812 naval battle between "Old Ironsides" and the *Guerrière.*

▶**The White House Historical Association: Burning of Washington**
Read about the British invasion of Washington, D.C., during the War of 1812.

Wisconsin Historical Society: The War of 1812
Learn about the War of 1812 and its history in Wisconsin.

annex—To add on or attach territory.

blockade—The closing off of an area by ships to prevent supplies from reaching it.

cavalry—Soldiers on horseback.

confederation—A union of states or American Indian nations.

Congreve rocket—A weapon developed by Sir William Congreve for the British military that was used in war. It was not always accurate, but its loud explosion was useful in scaring the enemy.

cutlass—A sword.

Democratic-Republican—A member of a political party who did not want a strong central government and favored going to war.

Embargo Act—A law passed by Congress in 1807 that cut off trade with other nations.

Federalist—A member of an early American political party who was in favor of a strong central government and was against going to war.

frigate—A medium-sized warship that carries guns on two decks.

impressment—The practice of stopping American ships in port and at sea and forcing the sailors to serve in the Royal Navy.

Lower Canada—The eastern part of the British colony in North America.

militia—Citizen soldiers who are called to fight in an emergency by the state governor; also the military group to which they belong.

nationalism—A feeling of loyalty and devotion to one's country.

Northwest Territory—The present-day states of Ohio, Michigan, Indiana, Wisconsin, and Illinois.

Orders in Council—British laws that prevented any neutral nation from trading with any European nation except through British ports and with British licenses.

poltroon—A cowardly person.

privateer—A privately owned armed vessel that has a license to attack, raid, and sink enemy merchant ships; also a man who serves on board one of these vessels.

regular army—Full-time soldiers.

secede—To withdraw from an organization, such as a political party or nation.

United Empire Loyalist—A colonist who lived in British North America and was a supporter of Great Britain and King George III.

Upper Canada—The western part of the British colony in North America; now Ontario.

War Hawk—A member of Congress who favored going to war.

Chapter 1. Washington Burning

1. David B. Mattern and Holly C. Shulman, eds., *The Selected Letters of Dolley Payne Madison* (Charlottesville: University of Virginia Press, 2003), p. 193. Reprinted with the permission of the University of Virginia Press.

2. Glenn Tucker, *Poltroons and Patriots, A Popular Account of the War of 1812, Volume 2* (Indianapolis: Bobbs-Merrill Company, Inc., 1954), p. 738.

3. Ibid., p. 424.

4. Mattern and Shulman, p. 192.

5. Anthony Pitch, "The Burning of Washington," *The White House Historical Association,* n.d., <http://www.whitehousehistory.org/08/subs/08_b04.html> (April 8, 2005).

6. *Daily National Intelligencer,* August 24, 1814, p. 1.

7. Robert Allen Rutland, *The Presidency of James Madison* (Lawrence: University Press of Kansas, 1990), p. 161.

8. Mattern and Shulman, p. 193.

9. Ibid.

10. Virginia Moore, *The Madisons* (New York: McGraw-Hill Book Company, 1979), p. 316.

11. Benson J. Lossing, *The Pictorial Field-Book of the War of 1812* (Somersworth, N.H.: New Hampshire Publishing Co., 1976), pp. 935–936.

12. Mattern and Shulman, p. 194.

13. Paul Jennings, "A Colored Man's Reminiscences of James Madison, *The White House Historical Association,* n.d., <http://www.whitehousehistory.org/08/subs/08_b01.html> (May 4, 2005).

14. Anthony S. Pitch, *The Burning of Washington: The British Invasion of 1814* (Annapolis: Naval Institute Press, 1998), p. 108.

15. George Robert Gleig, "A British Account of the Burning of Washington," *National Center for Public Policy Research,* n.d., <http://www.nationalcenter.org/BritishBurnWashington1814.html> (January 27, 2005).

16. Walter Lord, *The Dawn's Early Light* (New York: Norton & Co., 1972), p. 170.

17. Mary Stockton Hunter, "The Burning of Washington, D.C.," *The New–York Historical Society Quarterly Bulletin,* vol. 8, no. 1, April 1924, pp. 80–83.

18. Moore, p. 322.

19. Tucker, p. 740.

Chapter 2. A Brief History of the War of 1812

1. Walter R. Borneman, *1812, The War That Forged a Nation* (New York: HarperCollins, 2004), p. 57.

2. W.R. Wilson, "Tecumseh," *Historical Narratives of Early Canada,* 2004, <http://www.uppercanadahistory.ca/1812/19122.html> (April 18, 2005).

3. Pierre Berton, *The Invasion of Canada, Volume One: 1812–1813* (Boston: Little, Brown and Company, 1980), p. 68.

4. Borneman, p. 57.

5. "Epigrams: Peace and War," *The James Madison Center,* n.d., <http://www.jmu.edu/madison/center/main_pages/madison_archives/quotes/great/epigrams.htm> (July 15, 2005).

6. Berton, p. iii.

7. "The New England Threat of Secession," *TeachingAmericanHistory.org, Ashbrook Center for Public Affairs,* n.d., <http://teachingamericanhistory.org/library/index.asp?documentprint=430> (July 18, 2005).

8. Gene Towner, "Battle of Baltimore—The Troops," *Fort McHenry National Monument and Historic Shrine, Details of the Battle of Baltimore,* n.d., <http://www.bcpl.net/~etowner/bb2c.html> (January 25, 2005).

9. John R. Elting, *Amateurs, To Arms! A Military History of the War of 1812* (Chapel Hill, N.C.: Algonquin Books, 1991), p. 69.

10. Ibid.

11. "An Act to Encourage the Destruction of the Armed Vessels of War of the Enemy," *The Avalon Project at Yale Law School,* n.d., <http://www.yale.edu/lawweb/avalon/statutes/1812-04.htm> (May 3, 2005).

12. Berton, pp. 129–130.

13. Dave Stewart, "The Surrender of Hull at Detroit," *Hillsdale College, Documents in Military History, The American War of 1812,* n.d., <http://www.hillsdale .edu/personal/stewart/war/America/1812/North/1812-Post.htm> (May 11, 2005).

14. Glenn Tucker, *Poltroons and Patriots, A Popular Account of the War of 1812, Volume 1* (Indianapolis: Bobbs-Merrill Company, Inc., 1954), p. 191.

15. J. Mackay Hitsman, *The Incredible War of 1812, A Military History* (Toronto: University of Toronto Press, 1965), p. 127.

16. Pierre Berton, *Flames Across the Border: The Canadian–American Tragedy, 1813–1814* (Boston: Little, Brown and Company, 1981), p. 342.

17. Ibid., p. 341.

18. Theodore Roosevelt, *The Naval War of 1812* (Annapolis: Naval Institute Press, 1987), pp. 355–356.

19. Ibid., p. 355.

20. "Colored American Warriors," *West Virginia University,* n.d., <http://www.libraries.wvu.edu/delaney/ warrior.htm> (July 27, 2005).

Chapter 3. In Their Own Words:
American Soldiers and Sailors

1. Mary C. Gillett, *The Army Medical Department 1775–1818* (Washington, D.C.: United States Army Center of Military History, 1981), p. 163.

2. Ibid., p. 170.

3. "The Memoirs of Jarvis Hanks," *The Patriot Files,* n.d., <http://patriotfiles.com/article.php?sid=102> (May 10, 2005).

4. "Two Accounts From the Battle of Lundy's Lane," *Galafilm War of 1812,* n.d., <http://www.galafilm.com/ 1812/e/events/luncy_eyewit.html> (April 20, 2005).

5. "War of 1812—James C. Price letter," *Jessamine Historical Quarterly,* Nicholasville, Ky., volume 2, number 1, January 2003, pp. 5–6.

6. Ibid.

7. Glenn Tucker, *Poltroons and Patriots, A Popular Account of the War of 1812, Volume 1* (Indianapolis: The Bobbs-Merrill Company, Inc., 1954), pp. 232–233.

8. "War of 1812 Letters—John Hollyday," *Sandusky County Scrapbook, The Battle of Fort Stephenson,* n.d., <http://www.sandusky-county-scrapbook.net/FtSteph/SoldLtr.htm> (May 18, 2005).

9. William S. Dudley, ed., *The Naval War of 1812, A Documentary History, Volume 1, 1812* (Washington, D.C.: Naval Historical Center, Department of the Navy, 1985), pp. 589–590.

10. "Capture of the USS *Chesapeake,* 1813," *Hillsdale College, Documents in Military History, The American War of 1812,* n.d., <http://www.hillsdale.edu/personal/stewart/war/America/1812/Naval/1813-Chesapeake-Berry.htm> (May 11, 2005).

11. William S. Dudley, ed., *The Naval War of 1812, A Documentary History, Volume 2, 1813* (Washington, D.C.: Naval Historical Center, Department of the Navy, 1992), p. 562.

12. Elisabeth Wilson, "The Story of Stephen Decatur," *Founders of America of Virginia,* 2004, <http://www.foundersofamerica.org/decatur.html> (August 17, 2005).

13. John A. McManemin, *Privateers of the War of 1812* (Spring Lake, N.J.: Ho-Ho-Kus Publishing Company, 1992), pp. 183–190.

14. Bruce Felknor, ed., "A Privateersman's Letters Home From Prison," *American Merchant Marine at War, War of 1812,* n.d., <http://www.usmm.org/felknor1812.html> (August 11, 2005). Reproduced with the permission of Bruce Felknor.

15. John C. Fredriksen, *War of 1812 Eyewitness Accounts, An Annotated Bibliography* (Westport, Conn.: Greenwood Press, 1997), p. 179.

16. Reginald Horsman, *The War of 1812* (New York: Alfred A. Knopf, 1969), p. 54.

17. Fredriksen, p. 177.

Chapter 4. American Indian, British, and Canadian Stories

1. Pierre Berton, *Flames Across the Border: The Canadian-American Tragedy, 1813–1814* (Boston: Little, Brown and Company, 1981), pp. 26–27.

2. John Gellner, ed., *Recollections of the War of 1812, Three Eyewitnesses Accounts* (Toronto: Baxter Publishing Company, 1964), p. 6. Reproduced with the permission of the Baxter Publishing Company.

3. Ibid., p. 17.

4. Donald E. Graves, ed., *Merry Hearts Make Light Days* (Ottawa, Canada: Carleton University Press, 1993), p. 99. Copyright © DE Graves 1994.

5. Ibid., p. 175.

6. J. Mackay Hitsman, *The Incredible War of 1812, A Military History* (Toronto: University of Toronto Press, 1965), p. 33.

7. J.L. Neilson, trans., *Reminiscences of the War of 1812–14; Being Portions of A Diary of A Captain of the "Voltigeurs Canadiens" While on Garrison at Kingston, Etc.* (Kingston, Ontario: News Printing Co., 1895), p. 14.

8. "The War of 1812—Militia and Civilian Life," *Archives of Ontario,* n.d., <http://www.archives.gov.on.ca/english/exhibits/1812/militia.htm> (April 13, 2005).

9. Ibid.

10. Ibid.

11. Ibid.

12. William Wood, ed., *Select British Documents of the Canadian War of 1812, Volume 1* (Toronto: The Champlain Society, 1920), pp. 549–550.

13. Hitsman, pp. 206–207.

14. "African Nova Scotians in the Age of Slavery and Abolition, Admiral Cochrane's Proclamation," *Province of Nova Scotia Archives & Records Management,* n.d., <http://www.gov.ns.ca/nsarm/virtual/africanns/archives.asp?ID=114> (August 18, 2005).

15. "Alexander Cochrane," *Galafilm War of 1812,* n.d., <http://www.galafilm.com/1812/e/people/cochrane.html> (August 17, 2005).

16. Reginald Horsman, *The War of 1812* (New York: Alfred A. Knopf, 1969), pp. 149–150.

17. "Samuel Leech's Account of War at Sea," *Broadside,* n.d., <http://www.nelsonsnavy.co.uk/engagement2.html> (August 17, 2005).

18. "The War of 1812—Prisoners of War," *Archives of Ontario,* n.d., <http://www.archives.gov.on.ca/english/exhibits/1812/prisoners.htm> (August 12, 2005).

Chapter 5. In the Words of Civilians

1. "Mrs. Lydia B. Bacon's Journal 1812," *Central Michigan University, Clarke Historical Library,* n.d., <http://www.clarke.cmich.edu/detroit/bacon1812.htm> (August 23, 2005).

2. Ibid.

3. Ibid.

4. "The Burning of Buffalo–The War of 1812," *The Buffalonian,* n.d., <http://www.buffalonian.com/history/articles/180150/TheBurningofBuffalo.html> (August 24, 2005). Transcription from original text by Stephen R. Powell, Buffalonian.com–2003.

5. B. Drachman, "The Joshua Penny Website," n.d., <http://members.fortunecity.com/bdrachman/page47.jpg> (August 24, 2005).

6. William S. Dudley, ed., *The Naval War of 1812, A Documentary History, Volume 2, 1813* (Washington, D.C.: Naval Historical Center, Department of the Navy, 1992), pp. 260–261.

7. "Laura Secord Is Presented to the Prince of Wales," *Galafilm War of 1812,* n.d., <http://www.galafilm.com/1812/e/people/secord_speach.html> (March 2, 2005).

8. "Robert Dickson, 'Letter to the Commander in Chief of British Forces,' Quebec, Dec. 23d, 1812," *Central Michigan University, Clarke Historical Library,* n.d., <http://clarke.cmich.edu/nativeamericans/mphc/documentsofwarof1812/dickson208.htm> (August 24, 2005).

9. "Amelia Harris Tells of an Atrocity," *Galafilm War of 1812,* n.d., <http://www.galafilm.com/1812/e/people/ameliaharris.html> (May 11, 2005).

10. "Patrick Finan's War Recollections," *Galafilm War of 1812,* n.d., <http://galafilm.com/1812/e/people/finan2.html> (April 20, 2005).

11. "Journal of a British Army Officer's Wife During the War of 1812," *The War of 1812,* n.d., <http://www.warof1812.ca/wife.htm> (August 12, 2005).

Chapter 6. The War in Song and Poetry

1. Jayson Dobney, "Military Music in the European and American Tradition," *The Metropolitan Museum of Art, Timeline of Art History,* n.d., <http://www.metmuseum.org/toah/hd/ammu/hd_ammu.htm> (June 29, 2005).

2. Edwards Park, *Smithsonian,* "Our Flag Was Still There," July 2000, <http://www.smithsonianmag.si.edu/smithsonian/issues00/jul00/object_jul00.html> (July 11, 2005).

3. "The Star-Spangled Banner," *Smithsonian National Museum of American History,* n.d., <http://americanhistory.si.edu/ssb/6_thestory/6b_osay/main6b1a.html> (April 14, 2005).

4. Wallace House, *Ballads of the War of 1812 [Sound Recording]* (New York: Folkways Records, 1954), Album No. 48–3A, Side I, Band 7.

5. Ibid., Album No. 48–4A, Side I, Band 2.

6. Ibid., Album No. 48–4A, Side I, Band 1.

7. Ibid., Album No. 48–4A, Side I, Band 5.

8. Ibid., Album 48–4B, Side II, Band 2.

9. "British and Canadian Songs," *Galafilm War of 1812,* n.d., <http://www.galafilm.com/1812/e/people/song_brit_can_songs.html> (April 14, 2005).

10. William R. Wilson, "The War No One Lost," *Historical Narratives of Early Canada,* 2004, <http://www.uppercanadahistory.ca/1812/18121.html> (April 14, 2005).

11. Donald Graves, "Songs of the War of 1812," *The War of 1812,* n.d., <http://www.warof1812.ca/songs.htm> (May 11, 2005).

12. House, Album 48–3B, Side II, Band 3.

13. *Raise the Flag and Other Patriotic Canadian Songs and Poems* (Toronto: Rose Publishing Co., 1891), p. 27.

Chapter 7. Press Coverage of the War

1. Carol Sue Humphrey, *The Press of the Young Republic, 1783–1833* (Westport, Conn.: Greenwood Press, 1996), p. 85. Reproduced with permission of Greenwood Publishing Group, Inc., Westport, CT.

2. "Chronicles of Baltimore," *Webroots.Org Library,* n.d., <http://www.webroots.org/library/usahist/cobmd009 .html> (September 20, 2005).

3. "Declaration of the War of 1812, Washington *National Intelligencer,* 14 April 1812," *Hillsdale College, Documents in Military History, The American War of 1812,* n.d., <http://www.hillsdale.edu/personal/stewart/war/ America/1812/1812-Newspapers-Declaration.htm> (May 3, 2005).

4. Ibid.

5. The *Centinel of Freedom,* Newark, N.J., Tuesday, June 2, 1812, vol. 37, p.1.

6. Walter R. Borneman, *1812, The War That Forged a Nation* (New York: HarperCollins, 2004), p. 58.

7. Glenn Tucker, *Poltroons and Patriots, A Popular Account of the War of 1812, Volume 1* (Indianapolis: The Bobbs-Merrill Company, Inc., 1954), p, 306.

8. Ibid.

9. Humphrey, p. 92.

10. "Miscellaneous Statements," *Galafilm War of 1812,* n.d., <http://www.galafilm.com/1812/e/people/songs_misc .html> (April 14, 2005).

11. "Peace with Britain, *National Advocate,* 17 February 1815," *Hillsdale College, Documents in Military History, The American War of 1812,* n.d., <http://www.hillsdale.edu/ personal/stewart/war/America/1812/1815-Newspapers-Peace.htm> (May 3, 2005).

12. "More Heroines of the War of 1812," *Parks Canada— Fort George National Historic Site of Canada,* n.d., <http:// www.pc.gc.ca/lhnnhs/on/fortgeorge/ne/ne3_E.asp> (September 6, 2005).

13. Ferdinand Brock Tupper, "The Project Gutenberg E-book of *The Life and Correspondence of Sir Isaac Brock*," December 23, 2004, n.d., <http://www.gutenberg.org/files/14428/14428.txt> (June 3, 2005).

14. Borneman, p. 219.

15. Tucker, p. 581.

Chapter 8. Did Anyone Really Win?

1. John R. Elting, *Amateurs, To Arms! A Military History of the War of 1812* (Chapel Hill, N.C.: Algonquin Books, 1991), p. 327.

2. "Table 2-23, Department of Defense, Principal Wars in Which the United States Participated," United States Department of Defense, n.d., <http://web1.whs.osd.mil/mmid/m01/SMS223R.HTM> (September 20, 2005).

3. Donald R. Hickey, *The War of 1812, A Forgotten Conflict* (Chicago: University of Illinois Press, 1989), pp. 302–303.

4. Walter R. Borneman, *1812, The War That Forged a Nation* (New York: HarperCollins, 2004), p. 304.

5. Ibid., p. 328.

6. Hickey, p. 297.

7. Fred L. Engelman, *The Peace of Christmas Eve* (London: Rupert Hart-Davis, 1962), pp. 300–301.

8. William Wood, ed., *Select British Documents of the Canadian War of 1812, Volume 1* (Toronto: The Champlain Society, 1920), p. 132.

9. Hickey, p. 304.

10. Pierre Berton, *Flames Across the Border: The Canadian-American Tragedy, 1813–1814* (Boston: Little, Brown and Company, 1981), pp. 427–429.

11. Donald E. Graves, *The Battle of Lundy's Lane on the Niagara in 1814* (Baltimore: The Nautical & Aviation Publishing Company of America, 1993), p. 205.

12. Berton, p. 424.

Berton, Pierre. *Canada Under Siege.* Toronto: McClelland & Stewart, 1991.

Bramwell, Neil D. *James Madison: A MyReportLinks.com Book.* Berkeley Heights, N.J.: MyReportLinks.com Books, 2003.

Collier, Christopher, and James Lincoln Collier. *The Jeffersonian Republicans, 1800–1823: The Louisiana Purchase and the War of 1812.* New York: Benchmark Books, 1999.

Collier, James Lincoln. *The Tecumseh You Never Knew.* New York: Children's Press, 2004.

Crump, Jennifer. *The War of 1812 Against the States: Heroes of a Great Canadian Victory.* Canmore, Alberta: Altitude Publishing, 2003.

Fryer, Mary Beacock. *Bold, Brave, and Born to Lead: Major General Isaac Brock and the Canadas.* Toronto: Boardwalk Books, 2004.

Howes, Kelly King, and Julie L. Carnagie, eds. *War of 1812.* Detroit: UXL, 2002.

Kent, Zachary. *James Madison: Creating a Nation.* Berkeley Heights, N.J.: Enslow Publishers, Inc., 2004.

MacDonald, Cheryl. *Laura Secord: The Heroic Adventures of a Canadian Legend.* Canmore, Alberta: Altitude Publishing, 2005.

Pitch, Anthony. *The Burning of Washington: The British Invasion of 1814.* Annapolis: Naval Institute Press, 1998.

Shulman, Holly C., and David B. Mattern. *Dolley Madison: Her Life, Letters, and Legacy.* New York: PowerPlus Books, 2003.

Smolinski, Diane, and Henry Smolinski. *Soldiers of the War of 1812.* Chicago: Heinemann Library, 2003.

Stefoff, Rebecca. *The War of 1812.* New York: Benchmark Books, 2001.

Weitzman, David. *Old Ironsides: Americans Build a Fighting Ship.* Boston: Houghton-Mifflin, 2003.